When Anxiety Wants to Play Here's How We Win

**Turn the page,
the monster shrinks
when you do.**

WRITTEN BY: Israel Maya

Table of Contents

∾

This book was written by a real human...me. It came from my head, and hands based on my experiences of intense anxiety and all the wonderful techniques I learned and came up with to get rid of it. No AI helped. I promise.

Introduction

∞

I want you to imagine the following. It's a regular morning for you and the normal time you usually awaken. Your mind is calm, and a smile washes across your face. You tell yourself it's going to be a great day. Sitting up in bed, you reflect on the past and notice how much things have changed for the better from the old you. Your eyes gently close and a soft smile forms. You think about the person you were before and say, "That was me a long time ago, but I'm a new person now." Your door swings open when you are ready to leave the house. You look outside and see a deep blue sky where birds are chirping in the trees and a cool breeze is blowing. These are things you wouldn't notice before, but you do now. You take a deep breath, holding it for a few seconds. With a slow exhalation, eyes close before emphatically saying: "Today is going to be amazing!" What makes it so? You have no idea, but one thing is for sure: a calm, peaceful existence is part of who you are now. You are in control of your feelings and emotions. After getting home in the evening, you sit on the couch and reflect on the day. The corners of your mouth turn upward, and the inner monologue says, "Today was such a great day." Sure, there were stressful moments, but you handled each situation like a champ. Your eyes lower slightly, and you say, "Life is full of challenges, but they don't have to consume my every thought. I just take care of things as they come and preemptively do my best to prevent difficult situations I think may arise." As you lie in bed that night, your body has a serene feeling, knowing that when you awaken tomorrow, things are going to be just as terrific as they were today. You drift off into a deep, tranquil sleep with a big grin and forget about the world for a few hours as your body relaxes profoundly.

I've just described a pretty awesome day. I'm sure this is where you would want to be. Does anyone have as perfect a day as the one above? We both know the answer is no. What is consistent above, though, is that there is no anxiety. It's not running or controlling the above person's life. Sure, there are challenges; but neither you, me, nor the person above is immune to stressful situations. All of us get a scare from time to time, but how do we react when that happens? Do we hold on to the scare or let it go? Your answer to this and how you respond will make a world of difference in your life. Anxiety should not, and cannot, be part of our lives. (Notice how I include myself.) If it is, we are wasting precious time and losing it to a feeling that will never serve us. Keep in mind that most of the things that we get anxious or scared about in life **DO NOT HAPPEN**. Ever! Have you ever noticed that?

Without having to go out on a limb, I am sure you picked up this book because you suffer from anxiety that runs your life and are looking for a way out. Can you be that person who finds the way out? Can you get rid of anxiety? I know you undoubtedly can as you follow the suggestions in my book. How do I know? I used to have bad anxiety myself for many years. My anxiety started as far back as I can remember, which is the case for many people. I remember my mom saying, "He's just a nervous kid." This "nervousness" turned into mild anxiety, generalized anxiety with eventual full-blown panic attacks well into my 30s. I definitely had major separation anxiety as a child alongside many senseless fears. It was torture day in and day out. I had blocks of time where it was manageable, but it was always there and I was always on alert.

There was a constant low level of anxiety lurking in my emotional shadows like a thief in the night. At some point, I knew that terrible, gripping feeling was going to wrap itself around me, squeezing tighter and tighter, cutting off my air supply, making me wish I had never been born. My emotional being would turn blue, gasping for air, begging for respite. The fear of it coming made me anxious before the real feeling struck. I'd yell, "Why? Why me? What did I do to deserve this?" Of course, I'd never have an answer. It was at its worst when I'd get up in the middle of the night with a panic attack. My heart pounded, blood pressure rose, and breathing was fast-paced. The stillness of the late night made it all worse. I'd walk back and forth nervously as everyone else slept. My mind raced, as untamed thoughts certified death. "I'm going to die, Oh my God, I'm going to die." The grand finale was getting dizzy and weak, having to sit down. To bring myself to some sort of reality, I'd pacify my mind by saying, "I'm okay, I'm okay. It's going to be okay." When I wasn't overtaken by panic, I often felt an internal storm brewing with a crescendo that begged suppression. While this helped, it made matters worse as the lull led up to the next explosive attack.

Sound familiar? If you haven't experienced this, then most likely something like it. I know, I understand, and I empathize with you. It's a horrible feeling, and I wouldn't wish it upon anyone. I didn't deserve it, and neither do you. It's very hard to live like this, and if I can be a friend to you and put my arm around your shoulder, I'd say, "It's going to be okay." You can get out of this hole, and there is light at the end of the tunnel. It may not feel that way now, but you can and will get there. I did it without medication, helped others do it, and will help you too. I'll show you what I've learned and how I've worked with others to raise their awareness, understand, and get rid of their anxiety so you can do the same. You will understand anxiety in a way that others don't, minimize it, gain confidence against it, release it, and let it go. Strap in. Follow along, and let me guide you with what I've learned to help you get rid of anxiety once and for all. I wrote this book with a lot of love, heart, and passion. I hated having anxiety and couldn't stand when others had it either, so I did my utmost to help them. I will do the same here for you.

In this book, I'm going to give you bite-sized chapters. Some chapters will be quite short. This is being done intentionally so that you have the opportunity to read it and possibly reread it, digest the information, practice the techniques that are given, or really think about what was written. A lot of the information that I present to you here is common sense. This is something that we tend to lose when experiencing constant anxiety. We lose our common sense and become afraid of things that will never happen or ever harm us. Take in the ideas that follow on a deep level. Think about them logically; absorb them in your mind so that they can make an impression on you and give you the freedom that you deserve. Make sure to read everything presented to you with an open mind as the conscious mind tends to be dismissive of ideas that are in conflict with what it believes. This prevents growth. Don't stunt your growth. Keep an open mind.

Oh my goodness! In my enthusiasm to begin, I almost forgot to mention that all the information presented in this work is solely based on my personal opinion. Please don't consider anything written here as medical advice. I'm not a medical doctor, so before starting any new regimen that could potentially impact your current physical or mental health, it's advisable to consult your healthcare advisor, professional, or doctor.

One more thing. Anxiety can stem from chemical imbalances in the brain, severe physical, emotional trauma, or maybe even from medication. It's possible that the way you feel from certain life stressors or past experiences has already created an imbalance, and perhaps correcting those thought patterns may correct the anxiety. I don't know, as everyone is an individual. Then again, neither does anyone else. What does "generalized anxiety" mean when a doctor says it? It just means we don't know what the heck you have and don't know what to do about it. Here's a medication that will calm you down. They do the best they can; it's not their fault. (I'm being nice.) Keep in mind that there are no quick fixes, and there are no magic bullets. In this book, I do the best I can to give you everything I've used on myself first and with my past clients. Whether these techniques will work for brain and chemical imbalances, I can't say, but it's definitely worth a try. Finally, remember that as you feel better from using the techniques in this book or before starting, please seek guidance from or consult your health care provider concerning any discontinuing of medication. Those are sensitive issues and the advice from your practitioners is important in keeping balance. Oh yeah and another thing.

This book was <u>NOT</u> written by AI. It has the human touch as I wrote it myself. With all that in mind, let's go!

CHAPTER 1

Why We Get Anxious

∽

As we begin this journey together, I want you to have fun with what we do. If we don't have fun, then we're going to contribute to more negative feelings that you're already having. I understand that anxiety isn't fun, but what if we take a lighter approach so that we can whisk away the dark clouds that usually accompany this condition? Let's get some sunshine in here to dissipate the darkness. Agreed? Besides, you will see that as you reach a deeper understanding of anxiety, and what it truly is and isn't, you'll give it less and less importance, allowing you to enjoy your life more and more. (That last sentence is worth rereading.) Breathe it in and know that the more you understand what these feelings are about, the better your life is going to be and the quicker you'll be free.

There could be a myriad of reasons why you have anxiety. Some anxiety, as you probably already know, is necessary. Our main focus in this book, though, is obviously to work with the anxiety, which is unnecessary and the one that doesn't let us live our lives in a healthy way. There are many different types of anxieties, and we can't list all of them as everyone of us is a unique individual, each of us fearing different things. One thing our anxieties have in common, however, is that they are rooted in the subconscious mind. We have a conscious and subconscious mind. Our conscious mind is the logical part of us, and our subconscious contains the information of what we've learned since we were children, our behaviors, emotions, habits, and reactions. When we fear something, we have anxiety, a nervous reaction, or panic. It's not our conscious mind; it's our less-than-conscious mind, or subconscious. You see, our conscious, logical mind will give us a bunch of reasons why we shouldn't worry, be scared, or panic, and they all make sense, don't they? Ask yourself, is there any reason why I should get so anxious? The answer most of the time is no. Yet, we still do. Why? Why does the conscious part of us recede in the background, and the subconscious take over? It's almost automatic even though we know we shouldn't react this way. That unconscious part of our minds houses all of our habits, and get this, it is actually trying to protect us from something it believes is a threat. This is why we get anxious. Fear, anxiety, panic are all pretty much the same with varying degrees, but they are a protective factor to shield us from something our less-than-conscious mind believes is a threat. Going a little deeper, our experiences or belief system based upon what we've learned creates a narrative in our minds to indicate what is and isn't a threat, therefore becoming scared, stepping back, or running away. With that comes the symptoms of anxiety: racing heart, fast breathing, tightness in the stomach or chest, and illogical thinking.

Once we create the narrative which labels things as a threat, our bodies react to what we believe will hurt us, and we form a habit. With enough repetition, a habit eventually occurs without thought. In other words, the anxious response. Anxiety begins as either a logical or illogical response to something we perceive as a threat, eventually becoming an unconscious habit with automatic reactions. At times, we don't even know why we react the way we do because the reaction is unconscious.

Example of a logical response: Emma had a bad experience with a dog when she was four years old. While they were visiting her mother's friend, the dog barked and lunged at Emma, making her cry. Understandably, she may not want to interact with dogs after the initial experience, being scared of them. Whenever Emma sees dogs as an adult, she panics, staying as far away from them as possible. This example makes sense as Emma was only a child and thought this is what all dogs do. Although as an adult she may reason that all dogs are not harmful, she may have a lingering fear.

Example of an illogical response: Jay was five years old when he was told by his older cousin, Ryan, that when it thunders really loud, it means that something bad is going to happen. Ryan was only joking as he enjoyed watching his cousin get scared. Unfortunately, Jay took his cousin's words seriously, and every time he heard loud thunder, he would get panic attacks, thinking that something bad would literally happen. He was unsure as to what, but he expected a bad scenario. When Jay got older, he forgot what his cousin told him but was scared to leave his house when heavy thunderstorms were forecasted. Feeling fear became the norm when he heard thunder, yet he couldn't understand why.

Remember that the subconscious part of us contains our habits. Here's why. Let's use driving as an example. When we begin to drive, we have to think about practically everything we're doing. Push the pedal, step on the brake, look around for pedestrians, scan for cars, check the lights. It's overwhelming at the beginning, but with enough practice, it becomes second nature. The habit we form is a necessary strategy that prevents us from having to constantly think about every move we make to drive safely each time we drive, so receding repeated actions to the subconscious is very beneficial. We develop these automatic or unconscious responses about thousands of things. Brushing our teeth, tying our shoes, flossing, showering, brushing our hair. The list is endless, and this is how we are able to multitask. The problem is when we develop negative automatic unconscious habits like responding with fear, anger, depression, procrastination, apathy, or any unhealthy response. Just like we create positive habits, we create negative ones as well. The negative responses become just as habitual as our positive ones, and they then become difficult to uproot because they form our identity. In order to change those illogical things we perceive as scary, we have to work on them, and in this book, I will give you the tools. Just start with an open mind.

CHAPTER 2

Begin With a Clean Slate

∽

It's our tendency to compare similarities when we start something new. It's normal and makes us feel safe knowing that what we're about to embark on has some familiarity. Many people feel nervous starting something new because they don't know how they are going to react or what to expect, so finding familiarity brings comfort. We also tend to assume that when something is familiar to us, we already know what it's going to be about. Taking this approach means stopping the learning process because if I already know this, what am I going to learn? Be careful with this thinking, especially when learning the suggestion of this program. Here are a list of don'ts so that you don't undermine your own success.

Don't think that the techniques you are learning here are too easy and not effective enough. Sometimes the simplest or easiest of things can be the most powerful.

Don't believe that just because what you're reading in this work is similar to something you've done before, it's the same. We can sabotage our learning process thinking "I already know this." Instead, look at this with fresh eyes even if you've done something similar, or the same. You may just understand something you didn't in the past.

Don't get discouraged when you get anxious again. It's easy to get discouraged when doing this work if there is a fallback. This is normal, and we all have days where we take a few steps forward and one back (or two). Remember that it most likely took years to develop anxiety, and while we don't want to take years to get rid of it, it does take time. The important thing is to keep working at it and not give up.

Don't beat yourself up because you have anxiety, fears, or nervousness. You never asked for this. You never woke up one day and said, " I want to be an anxious person." Right now, it's your nature or your programming. We are working hard to change what has become your nature. It's not easy, but it is doable.

Don't make yourself feel bad by saying "I was perfectly fine yesterday, and now I'm anxious." "What is wrong with me! " "Why do I have to continue having this battle and this fight?" Keep working at it, and you'll get rid of it. Things will get better and better with time as you work at it. It has to because you are working toward changing your internal programming.

Be Patient
As mentioned before, it took time to get here, so it's going to take time to get out. The amount of time depends on how much you are willing to invest. The more time you put into it, the faster you are going to heal. If you want awesome results, you have to put time into letting go of anxiety every day. Hey, anxiety is persistent, and you should be too. As you already know, Rome wasn't built in a day, so anxiety won't be toppled over in a day either. It will take time to understand what anxiety is, chip away at it, learn the techniques that I will teach you, and put them into practice. What you will experience though is more self-confidence as you gain more knowledge. Although by the end of this book we will learn that anxiety is not the enemy (and there aren't any), you will be able to accept anxiety for what it is and release it so that you gain control of your emotions and life. Just be patient and do the best you can to enjoy the process. You are on your way to becoming a better version of yourself. Own it and live it!

CHAPTER 3
Why is this happening to me?

∽

This is a difficult question and one that shows great distress. When we are in pain, it's our tendency to ask "Why is this happening to me?" or "Why is God doing this to me?" When we are sick or in pain, we can take some kind of medication, and after a day or a few, we feel better and all is forgotten. This isn't the case with constant anxiety though. It's always there even if you feel better. It lurks, hovers, or hides in the shadows. We distract ourselves and forget that it's there sometimes, or suppress it, but who are we kidding? It's still there, right? Anxiety comes from an already agitated mind. If you ask the above questions, they don't serve any purpose other than to temporarily release tension, but it just agitates the mind more. This is because we never get a proper answer with the above questions. Why is this happening to me? Who the heck knows? One can come up with a myriad of reasons, weighing heavily on the mind. Not that this is a religious book by any means, but many ask: "Is God punishing me?" Who knows the mind of God? I don't believe that God punishes neither you, me, nor anyone else. I think we punish ourselves. Plus, this is a bad place to go to unless you communicate directly with the Creator, which I would imagine is not the case. The answers we get from these types of questions not only agitate the mind more, it also means you have no control over your anxieties and the circumstances that surround it. When you lack control over something that is bothersome, you feel stuck, and stuck is never a good place to be as it causes more frustration and, yep, you guessed it, more anxiety.

We cannot be satisfied with asking a question that we have no answer for, so instead of asking those types of questions, ask ones that will give you an answer. Ask how? What? How can I get out of this? What can I do right now to feel better? Can I let this feeling go? Is it possible to let this feeling go? You may not have the answer at this moment, but you will as you go through my book. There are other things that need to be explained first; it's not that I want to keep you in suspense. In any case, let's dive into what anxiety really is.

CHAPTER 4

What is Anxiety?

Before I answer this question, I want to remind you to keep an open mind. Understanding what anxiety is from a different perspective will help to put things into a more manageable point of view. Your regular textbook definition of anxiety is intense, excessive, or persistent worry. As we mentioned before, it's always there, pestering you and gnawing away at your brain. It causes many symptoms, like your classic fast heartbeat, rapid breathing, and a tensing of the body. It's exhausting, isn't it? I remember that having constant anxiety for me would just wear me out. I longed for the day where I wouldn't feel it. For many people, maybe even for you, anxiety is a big, scary monster waiting to jump and scare the living daylights out of you.

By the way, with what I'm about to say, I don't want you to feel that I'm invalidating your feelings. I know what anxiety is; I lived it and it's very unpleasant, so don't think I don't understand because I do. I just want you to look at anxiety from a different angle to give you the upper hand.

Here's the way I see it, my friend: Anxiety, worry, fear, nerves... are just a ghost, a phantasm. That's the way I like to perceive it. Those feelings don't exist. They feel very real, but there's nothing there. I like to compare anxiety to the steam that comes off of hot food. It's there, it looks like something you can grab, but when you try, your hand goes right through it. You can try and hold it all you want, but you'll always have nothing once you open your hand. To further highlight how anxiety is an illusion, think about this for a moment. You can feel great one moment, where nothing is wrong, you're having a good time, and all of a sudden, anxiety strikes. It hits you, and you say, "Oh no, not now, please not again." The more you worry about it, the more it grows. It intensifies and begins to wrap itself around you like a Burmese python squeezing harder and harder. But how did you get there? How did this happen? It happened with a thought, maybe conscious, maybe subconscious. Either way, most of the time, there is no harm that is coming to you other than what you conceive in your mind. Right now, as you read this book, ask yourself: Is everything okay? If nothing bad is going on around you (which I hope not), then your answer should be, "Yes, everything is okay." Your mind is engaged, it's focused on my question, and most likely calm. However, if you begin to think about your fears, your body tenses, and you go into panic mode.

This is all generated by your mind, your imagination, the master of illusion. Are things which are imagined real? (All spirituality aside.) How do you answer that question? What does your mind say? (Stop reading and think about it.) What answer did you get? No? That's the right answer. Imagined things are just in your mind; imagined thoughts have no physical manifestation. It could be a picture in your mind or the semblance of an image. This is not real. It's the same as when you begin to think anxious thoughts. They are not real. They are just thoughts, a figment of your imagination. An anxious thought may be based on reality; for example, if you have to take a test tomorrow and you are worried about how well you're going to do. This is reasonable. The problem is that as you feed the anxiety monster, it grows and gets bigger and bigger, causing your body to respond with stress. To dig deeper, anxiety can be based on reality from trauma. This is more involved than just taking a test. If you have experienced an emotionally distressing event, the event may play in your mind over and over again, causing more anxiety. Once the event is over, and you replay the event in your mind, it is no longer real.

It is again, imagined and a figment of your imagination at that point based on a real event. Additionally, there may be significant emotion attached to this incident, and your mind will use this emotion to protect you from any future threats that may relate to it.

With either example going from less to more extreme, the intensity of the emotion may vary, but the inner mechanisms that push your anxious feelings are the same. They can be dealt with in the same fashion.

Anxiety is a feeling that you get when you begin to incessantly and unnecessarily worry about something. The more it intensifies, the closer you get to the pinnacle, which is the panic attack. Those are never fun because once in this zone, you lose control over your emotions, and the inevitable thought comes into mind, which is "I'm going to die." If you've had enough panic attacks, you eventually learn that you're not going to die based on the fact that you're not dead from the last group of attacks. Nonetheless, if the subconscious mind feeds you with the idea that you're going to die, you'll feel that way. Take a breath. Relax. If you haven't died by now from panic attacks, then chances are really high that you're not going to if you have another one. Does that bring you comfort? Think about it. Does it comfort you to know that the panic will pass and you'll still be alive? It should. As horrible as the feeling is when you go through it, there is a comfort to know that another side exists which is much brighter than the one you were in. I want you to really think about it. Does it give you comfort to know that? If you said yes, then you've just experienced getting out of the illusion. Pay attention to how your body responds, and feel the peace. You used your mind to make you feel better, and knowing that lets you in on the very important fact that you, yes, you have the capacity to control your feelings and emotions. There can be outside, or subconscious factors that control your responses, but ultimately your mind has the power to willingly be at peace. You choose which part of you is going to control that. If you don't choose, then a default mental program will take over, most likely being anxiety. You have to change that because it's become a habit. The power rests in your hands.

CHAPTER 5

Your Most Powerful Tool

∾

The pharmaceutical companies have created incredible drugs that can influence practically every part of our body. They also have drugs that can greatly affect our minds by altering brain chemistry, causing a shift in depression or anxiety, making things seem more peaceful. This being said, as a side note, I am not advocating for or against any pharmaceutical drug. Again, they are wonderful, and when used in the right time and for the right purpose, they are very effective and many times life-saving. It becomes problematic when we rely too much on them as opposed to relying more on ourselves and the power we have within us. In the case of anxiety, the capacity to control it, let it go, or get rid of it forever rests in the power of our own minds. There may be individuals who will need to be on medication for some time in their lives for anxiety, and that's okay. The real question is, does that drug really address the underlying problem? This is what, regardless of whether you choose to medicate or not, you must keep in mind and consider aside from the side effects. If the medication does not address the underlying difficulty, then you will need to do everything possible to address it properly at some point, and one of the most powerful ways is doing it with your mind.

Your mind is the single most important tool you will ever need (with the right guidance) to eradicate anxiety. Why? Well, as we stated above, anxiety or any feeling that surrounds it comes from the mind. It conjures up the feelings, stirs the pot, so to speak, and puts you in code red with alarms and flashing lights even when nothing harmful is happening. When we truly understand this, we can also come to the realization that even though the mind is creating the anxiety, it must also conversely be true that the mind is the antidote which can stop anxious thoughts. Simply put, if it can give it, it can put an end to it. We also realize that anxiety is coming from the inside out, not the converse. Many people believe that anxiety is the cause of an outside factor. This may be true at the onset, but for the most part, the thoughts fueling the feeling must come from the inside out. (Thoughts cannot come from the outside.)

In order to get rid of anxiety, you must be open to the awareness that you and only you have the power to release the thoughts and feelings that are imprisoning you. You are the only one that can make this happen, even if you are working with a professional who has helped millions of people. That person does not have any power to make you release anxiety; this book and my methods don't have that ability either; only you have it. We only serve as guides to put you on the right track, but you, in essence, have to do the work and make the choice whether or not you want to continue holding on to anxiety or let it go. I know it's a big responsibility to put on your shoulders, but that's the way it is. This is because only we as individuals have the power to control ourselves, and that's a good thing. We only allow other things to control us if we let them, but once you say "no" to it, and yes to you, with the realization that you are in control, then whatever has been trying to influence you loses its power, and you take charge moving forward.

Just reading this should give you some comfort even if you haven't learned a single technique. Does it make you feel any better? It's good to recognize even the slightest shift because here again you are witnessing that your mind creates an illusion to which you respond. The illusion in this case is the good feeling you get from understating that you can choose. There's nothing wrong with choosing and having good feelings, but know that pleasant and unpleasant feelings are illusions because they fade. Your mind causes you to feel better knowing that you have the power to choose. One minute you feel good, but then something happens and you feel bad. What is consistent is that you are the one who makes the choice to either have a positive or negative response based on what you are feeding your mind, what you hear, see, or think. Once you understand and internalize this, you come to realize that even if you are feeling jumpy or anxious it is just a passing fancy and a peaceful feeling is just around the corner because it's actually always present. Come and explore this concept with me in the next chapter.

CHAPTER 6
Where is Peace?

∾

There is an apparent derived quote from Confucius, saying, "A healthy person has a thousand dreams, while a sick person has only one. The original quote may be, "A healthy person has a thousand wishes, but a sick person has only one." Either way, the idea is the same. When you are well physically and mentally, you can dream and wish for so many things without getting bogged down with the obsessive focus on illness. If you are not well, getting better is all you think about, robbing you of your ability to dream or have desires. Anxiety does the same thing to you. It strips you of your wishes to think beyond the constant worry and puts thought patterns in an endless loop of negative thinking patterns, which affect the body, mind, and everyday life. Ayyy, this sucks!

So where is peace? How can you achieve finding or feeling peace when anxiety gets in the way or is part of everyday thinking? The answer is easier than you think, although it will require some explanation. Peace is right where you are and the only real feeling that exists. In order to explain this, I want to steer you away with a comparison of sound. We'll compare sounds to negative feelings, and the absence of sound or silence to peace.

Let's say you are in a quiet room and all of a sudden you hear an ambulance or police car speed by with the sirens blaring. We believe the silence is "broken or gone" as your ears hear the siren, right? As soon as the emergency vehicle is far enough away and you no longer hear the siren, what remains? The silence, right? The siren faded in and out as a result of the ambulance or police car passing by, but the silence didn't leave; you just couldn't hear it because the siren was louder than the silence and took your focus away from it, yet the silence remained. You were distracted from the silence when the noise occurred. One thing is consistent when there are no sounds, and that is silence. Silence is ever present and real. Noise, that which seemingly breaks silence, is an illusion because it doesn't last. It is momentary. The same holds true for anxiety or any negative feeling. Once the energy of that feeling is gone, what remains in the background to be reclaimed is peace. The human being wants to be in physical and psychological homeostasis, and this only occurs when there are no feelings or emotions that create physical or mental stress. When certain occurrences in life "push our buttons," they create mental chaos, and we get knocked off our peaceful horse. When the chaos dissolves, we return to our natural, peaceful state.

Let's take another example. For those who drive, this will have happened to you plenty of times. You're driving along the road, and everything is fine. You are as calm as can be, smile on your face, maybe singing along with a favorite tune on the radio when all of a sudden someone cuts you off. You jump in your seat; your heart races, and after the fear wears off, you get angry, wanting to give the other driver a piece of your mind. You yell, you scream with the feeling lingering for a few minutes, but once the person drives away or when you realize it's not worth getting upset over, you calm down. You then resort back to the peaceful feelings you had prior to the scare, albeit with your eyes on the lookout.

So you see? The peace you are searching for when trying to rid yourself of any anxious feelings exists within you all the time and never actually leaves you. You just have to know:

1. that peace is always there
2. how to access it

Besides, if you are doing well and try to look for negative feelings, you won't be able to find them. Try right now to look for a feeling that is not being caused by chaotic thinking. For example, if you have no reason to feel jealous at this moment, try and search for a feeling of jealousy to see if you can find it. Don't think of something that could make you jealous, just try in vain to find that feeling, and you'll realize it's not there. Most likely your mind will reject the fact that you are jealous and maybe challenge why you are trying to look for jealousy. Try and do the same thing with any feeling that is not there, and you'll see you can't find it. You know how these feelings feel, and yes, you can conjure them up with your imagination, but are they there? If the negative feelings aren't there, then what is? You'll find that the answer is peace, and once again, peace is something that is real; it already exists within you because you don't have to look for it; it's already there.

I want you to sit with this and really think about the important message this chapter is giving you. Basically, anxiety is an illusion because it is short-lived, and the motive for feeling anxious eventually dissolves and disappears every time, in healthy individuals, and even faster when you get distracted.

We will learn to let go of feelings that are superimposed on top of your personal peace so that you can let any negative feeling go. For now, let's keep eroding the belief system about anxiety and continue to chip away at its foundation so that we can watch it crumble.

CHAPTER 7

Why am I so anxious?

∞

Did you ever ask yourself that question? Probably a bunch of times, right? Why? Why don't you know the reason? Why do you have to ask yourself the reason for anxiety? There are times where you have an answer. "I have a test tomorrow," "I'm meeting with my boss for a raise," "I have to speak to my friend about a sensitive matter." Those have justification, but I'm talking about the "general anxiety" that eats away at you on a daily basis. It's that jittery feeling you get when your mind begins to run wild with thoughts. It's the feeling that resides somewhere in your stomach or chest. It may cause you to shake your leg, dart your eyes, run away from others, or pace back and forth. As we've said before, it's a feeling that lurks inside of you like a thief in the shadows waiting to strike. It may be under control for now, but you know that little feeling which may currently seem harmless can grow and pester you until you get the gripping anxiety which leaves you frozen or makes you feel like you want to jump out of your skin. Why is that there? Most of the time, people don't know, and when it's been around longer than they can remember they may not even care to know why. They just want to get rid of it, so they suppress it by distraction or medication. They'll do anything just to get through the day.

I'll tell you why your anxiety is there if you don't have an answer. It's there because you have some past issue that hasn't been resolved yet. Your subconscious is protecting you from something it considers a threat. Yes, I know I've said this before, but you need to hear it. This way you won't buy into the lie that says "I'm just an anxious person." No, you're not! This is not who you are. You're just reacting to a program in your mind that you feel is harmful. It's only harmful in your head, and as much as you may or may not want to hear it....it's an illusion, a ghost, a phantasm. It's something that will only hurt you in your imagination.

Keep in mind that if you repeat a pattern, whether thought or action, it becomes a habit, so anxiety that you experience may be based on the repeated anxious patterns you've played out throughout the years. Repeated actions or ways of thinking become a habit. Remember that when we do things repeatedly, the action eventually recesses to the subconscious part of us so that we don't have to think about it, i.e. driving a car, tying your shoes, brushing your teeth, etcetera. These are good, but having a constant negative reaction that is coming up because of subconscious programming doesn't serve us in the least bit. We have to create a new program in place of the one that is currently running in our less-than-conscious thinking.

So how are we going to do this? What can you possibly do to change who you are? All good questions, right? There are several things that can be done, and we will describe them beginning with the next chapter.

CHAPTER 8

Hypnosis

One of the most powerful ways to get rid of anxiety that I know of is hypnosis. I know, I'm a hypnotherapist, and I've seen my patients' anxiety practically vanish in a matter of 2 or 3 sessions. We've mentioned the subconscious in previous chapters, and we've learned that it is the place that houses your habits, emotions, feelings, etc. When you are very young, your mind is fertile ground, and it accepts every idea that it is told. It will believe everything, no matter how logical, illogical, forwards, or backwards. Once programming is accepted, the subconscious works automatically and behind the scenes to help you live your life and create an identity based upon the ideas and philosophies you've received from your parents, caretakers, friends, family members, and teachers. You acquire your identity from anyone and everyone who has had an influence on you, and the things you've experienced and seen, thus creating who you are. Once ideas enter and are accepted by the subconscious part of your mind, they are reinforced by similar things you experience in life and are protected so that you are able to keep your identity intact.

On the other hand, the conscious mind, or the part of the mind you are using right now, is the logical and rational part of your mind that analyzes everything. This part of your mind will tell you what is and isn't logical based upon what you have learned and have accepted in your subconscious. It will weigh options and scrutinize every idea it comes into contact with, dismissing what it doesn't agree with again based upon what programming you have in your subconscious mind. The conscious part of your mind also becomes the protector of the subconscious when it carefully examines and either accepts or rejects all the ideas it hears. It accepts what you already believe to be true and rejects those concepts you are not in agreement with as a means of keeping your identity intact.

When you do hypnosis, with a qualified hypnotherapist, you cut right through conscious thinking and bypass critical thought with the aim of discovering why you are anxious, going directly to the root cause. In other words, a hypnotherapist can work directly with the subconscious part of the mind and ask, "Take me back to the first time you experienced this anxiety," and you will instantly find yourself in an earlier time that has everything to do with the anxiety. This brings you a deeper understanding of why you react the way you do without the resistance to change or heal. When you work with the subconscious directly, you can ask it to stop reacting in an anxious way because whatever you accepted in the past is no longer a threat, and the less-than-conscious part of the mind will listen since it accepts suggestions without judgment when it believes the suggestion is beneficial.

In the past, unfortunately, movies painted a very negative outlook on hypnosis, making it appear as if the hypnotized person could be controlled by the operator. This is only true if the person either likes or wants to be controlled. In addition, hypnosis was not understood as well when those movies were made as it is now, yet the stigma remained. What is more true is that the hypnotized person always maintains their mental and physical control. Also, keep in mind that a hypnotized person is NOT asleep and can either accept or reject suggestions that are given by the operator. The difference in this and a "regular" mental state is that the mind doesn't scrutinize suggestions it knows will be beneficial, like letting go of fear or anxiety. While hypnotized, you can still be logical, just not as critical as in a non-hypnotized state.

What is hypnosis, you ask? It's basically a relaxed state of the mind where you can bypass excessive logical thinking. Interestingly enough, everyone experiences states of hypnosis every single day. You see, hypnosis is merely a brain wave state that you enter when you are going to sleep and when you are waking up. There are several brain wave states, and the hypnotic one is called theta, which again we pass through as we fall asleep and when we wake up. The difference is that while you are drifting off to sleep, you don't hold on to the theta or hypnotic state, and when you wake up, the same happens. You pass the state and move on to either falling asleep or waking up. When you work with a hypnotherapist, he or she can help you hold on to that theta state so you don't fall asleep allowing you to access your subconscious, understand what you're holding on to, and release the anxiety.

There's obviously more to it than just the above explanation, but basically, that's it. BUT, (and there's always a but) hypnosis works wonders for many, just not all. There are some people that believe or are convinced they cannot be hypnotized, and many of them resist. If I had $1 for every person that told me their mind was too strong to be hypnotized, I'd be...well, you know. Turns out, those people were pretty surprised when they were coming out of a deep hypnotic state. Many people have success in having hypnosis as they let go of resistance; unfortunately, some don't because they can't get past letting go. The resistance to hypnosis is a person's inability to let go because they are either too scared of what might happen, don't fully understand the process, and again are fearful of it, or they simply don't want to lose control, which again is trepidation wrapped up in a different way. It's a shame when a person comes to a hypnosis session and just doesn't let go because there are so many benefits to a successful hypnosis, and while hypnosis is not a cure-all for anxiety, it can fast-track many people to great relief.

Nonetheless, with those individuals who are not able to let go enough and enter a hypnotic state, I've given them the understanding and techniques that are taught in this book, and they've had great success in ridding themselves of anxiety with a bit more effort, work, and time. How long depends on your willingness to accept the suggestions written in this book. Since you now have a deeper understanding as to how the mind works, you are better equipped to change the programming in your subconscious. The less resistance you have to an idea or set of ideas, the more able you are to accept them and make the subconscious changes necessary to rid yourself of anxiety so that you can live a happier and more peaceful life. In the chapters that follow, we are going to learn how to use techniques to let go of anxious feelings, whether you've experienced hypnosis or not. The techniques are easy to use and give you instant results when used properly.

CHAPTER 9
Let It Go

ᕲᕣ

Do you have the song in your head now? I did when I started this chapter, but it's a good message to have in mind for the work we are doing. Now that you understand what anxiety is (an illusion), you are ready to begin letting it go. In this chapter, we are going to learn how to identify where the anxiety is and to release it with a simple yet powerful technique to free up the feelings that bottle up inside you when you feel anxious. I've used this technique on myself and with hundreds of others to help let go of any negative feelings within minutes, and I'm going to teach you to do the same. Exciting, right? Follow me as we take this step by step.

First, a basic understanding of feelings and how they are connected to the physical body. When you feel any positive or negative feeling, the thoughts (coming from your subconscious mind and reinforced by your conscious mind) generate a feeling in your body: the stomach, chest, or both. You may feel discomfort in other parts of your body like your neck or shoulders because of tension, but feelings are generated in the center of the body. Let's discover this in real time. I want you to close your eyes and think of something that makes you feel uncomfortable. While you are thinking of that thing, pay attention to the center region of your body and notice how that feeling bubbles up. When you feel the discomfort, stop thinking about it, let it go, and open your eyes coming back to me. Go ahead and do that now.

Did you notice any pressure, nausea, tightness, discomfort, or anything similar to this in your stomach or chest? If you did, it's good since you are able to identify where it is manifesting. These are the feelings we label as "bad." Now, let's do the opposite. I want you to do the same thing, but this time think of something pleasant. Don't hold back. Close your eyes, think of something that makes you feel good, putting you in an amazing mood, and notice what's happening in the center of your body. Pay attention to subtle, or distinct differences. Come back to me when you are ready.

Welcome back. Did you notice the difference in feeling? Negative thoughts produce an uncomfortable tightness or pressure, while positive thoughts generate an openness and expansive feeling. We label these as "good" or "bad," respectively. Besides the simplistic "good" or "bad," we also classify these feelings as happy, sad, scared, anxious, jealous, etc., as our brain interprets feelings and designates them based upon our past experiences with them. For example, if we learned that certain situations in life are supposed to make us mad, we say "I'm mad," when we learn sad we say "I'm sad," or scared we say "I'm scared." When referring to different types of negative feelings, though we label them with different names, their physical responses are similar. For example, anger, anxiety, fear, and conversely, excitement all release stress hormones, which cause the body to dump adrenaline, the heart rate to go up, and blood pressure to rise. You see? Different feelings with similar physical responses. Excitement is labeled "good," and the rest are labeled "bad." Doesn't that make you wonder what anxiety truly is? Real or just an illusion based on a label? Plus, it's a generated feeling in your body produced by thoughts. Please keep in mind as I mentored before and will remind you that I'm not invalidating your feelings. I know anxiety is uncomfortable; I've lived with it. I'm simply giving you a different understanding of it so that it doesn't have a hold on you. The more you understand something, the less scary it is. Surely you've experienced this in your life. When you finally do something that you thought may've been scary or difficult, you end up saying "that wasn't so bad," after you are done. Can you think of a time that happened to you? Now make a mental note and realize that you replaced the power you gained with the fear you had. This is how we conquer anxiety:

- Understand it.
- Break it down.
- Realize it's not as bad as we believed it to be.
- Let it go.

A Deeper Dive
Let's dive deeper to understand the above. When feelings in our bodies are negative, we shut down; when they are positive, we open up. In reality, there is only one response from the body, and that is resistance. Just like silence, which is ever-present, our natural desired state is to be at peace, which means open and flowing without bottling feelings. Unfortunately, when we experience life's difficult situations, our minds create negative scenarios, causing our body's energy to shut down, thereby resisting and denying ourselves the right to our natural openness.

Did I lose you? It may be easier to imagine than explain, so imagine that there is a doorway in the center of your body that extends from your chest to your stomach, which when open creates this expansive feeling we spoke about earlier. It prevents the bottling up of any negative feelings as unhindered feelings flow in and out of your body. When negative things happen in our lives, we close that door in an effort to protect ourselves and, in doing so, stop the flow of feelings from leaving us. Protecting ourselves is necessary, but when we do this, we trap undesirable feelings inside. If negative feelings don't flow out of our bodies, they build, causing tremendous pressure and discomfort. This feeling you feel inside of you is the anxiety. The mind's role in all of this is to generate thoughts that obsessively repeat themselves, creating the feeling. Thoughts go like a merry-go-round in an all-consuming way with what can and can't happen, which ends up affecting your body.

Let's break it down even further.

1. You encounter a negative occurrence in your life.
2. This creates a pessimistic thought which you hold on to.
3. The thoughts cause you to close the door as your body reacts to protect itself and generate negative feelings.
4. The negative feelings get trapped inside of you, causing more discomfort, which causes the door to be shut tighter.
5. You generate more incessant negative thoughts, which create more bad feelings.

There's no doubt this has happened to you in the past, although you may not know or pay attention to what the exact process is. You just say to yourself, "I'm upset!" A familiar and shortened version of this is when we argue with someone. Think about the last time you argued with a friend or loved one and couldn't get your point across. The center part of your body shuts down, and you almost feel helpless. The pressure increases in your stomach, chest, or both, and the more you argue, the worse it feels. When it's all over (if you settled your differences or walked away), you feel a release of pressure. It's like there's an automatic pressure release valve that opens, and you're at peace again. If we are able to release negative feelings, all is good, but when we learn to hold on to them, it creates an almost unbreakable cycle, which eventually leads to anxiety and a host of other negative feelings.

By the way, I know there isn't really a door in your body that swings open and closed to release or trap feelings, but as you saw above, the imagination is an integral part in creating feelings that cause discomfort, so in our wisdom, we use the imagination to counteract these negative feelings in order to return to peace. You can call it a door, trapped energy, or a muscle spasm; it doesn't matter. The use of a door (or if you want a window) is easy on the imagination. Smart, right? By the way, if you pay attention, you'll find that there is a tendency for humans to shrink or make themselves smaller when faced with a threat or certain level of discomfort, so the above-mentioned process is based upon actual physical responses. There are, of course, mental and physical reactions, and the mental ones require the imagination, which we need to start using to our advantage in order to rid the self of anxiety. We will also learn how to incorporate physical actions to break the anxiety cycle in an upcoming chapter.

For now, use your mind in order to let go of anxiety or, again, any negative feeling. We are going to outline the process of letting go in the next chapter. I really want you to understand the above concepts because they are invaluable and fundamental in letting go of negative feelings. I would even say reread this chapter to create a deeper understanding.

CHAPTER 10

How to Let it Go

∽

Did you reread the previous chapter? If you didn't, I really urge you to read it slowly, soaking in all of the concepts so that you can deepen your understanding of what is to come. Okay. Let's learn how to let anxiety go. As previously mentioned, you can use this method to let go of any feeling, but we are going to focus on anxiety since this book is about anxiety, isn't it?

To recap a little. Anxiety is unpleasant, right? It's not a feeling that you enjoy. At the same time, it's a feeling you unknowingly hold on to because you don't know that giving it an escape is possible.

Question: Where is this feeling trapped?
Answer: The stomach, chest, or both.

In order to let go of that feeling, you have to know it's possible to release, want to release it, and take the necessary steps to do so. If you are solid with the aforementioned, you will be successful; if not, the feeling is going to stay put.

Question: How do we release said feeling?
Answer: With an imaginary window or door large enough to cover your stomach, chest, or both, depending on where you feel it.

Question: Why do we use the imagination?
Answer: The imagination is used to create a pessimistic story in our minds, which in turn causes anxiety. We use the imagination to counteract the same feeling it produces.

Here's the theory: As we mentioned before, you are going to use your mind and the wonderful imagination that's available to you in order to let go of anxiety since anxiety stems from the imagination itself. Right? Good. Then we are going to give our feelings' center (stomach, chest, or both) an opening so that whatever feelings are accumulating there can flow out of your body. Keep in mind that you and I both know that this is just an image of the mind, it's an illusion, but then again, so is anxiety. Nonetheless, despite it being imaginary, we are going to use it to our advantage. I say this so many times because the mind's tendency is to dismiss the effectiveness of what we are about to do before commencing. This is called self-sabotage, and sadly, we do it to ourselves quite too often unless we are aware of it. We even do it to ourselves when we are aware of it, so imagine when we are not. Anyway, let's begin.

The Process of Letting Go
I want you to get comfortable and follow along with me exactly as I outline it. First, you are going to think of something that makes you anxious. You may think that this is counterproductive, but if you don't access the feeling, you are not going to learn how to let it go. Makes sense, right? When you have that feeling, you are going to close your eyes and imagine placing a window or door in the chest, stomach, or both and open it. Imagine that the feeling is leaving your body through the opening. Notice how you feel as you release and do your best to enjoy the process as opposed to judging it. After you have released the feeling, notice if there is any residual. Ask yourself: "Is there more to release and if there is can I let it go?" Notice the answer you get, or any resistance. If you tell yourself that you can't let it go, then ask yourself: " Why can't I let it go?" Remember in chapter 3 when we talked about questions we ask ourselves which we don't have an answer for? Why is this happening to me? What did I do to deserve this? No answer. It's frustrating. We have to engage in questions that have an answer. "Can I let this go?" Since you

already know you can, the answer is always "yes." We stimulate the mind to engage and guide it in the process of letting go. It also makes you feel better knowing you are in control of the anxiety and it's not in control of you. Most people think that anxiety is the one in control. When you take back your control, you are in charge. After going through the process, continue asking yourself if there is any residual until you don't feel any. Let's run through the actual process. I suggest you do it now. No better time than the present, right?

The Process Enumerated

1. Think of something that makes you feel anxious.
2. Notice an uncomfortable feeling manifesting in your stomach, chest, or both.
3. Close your eyes and imagine putting an opening in the affected area, and open it.
4. Allow the feeling to leave.
5. Reevaluate and see if you need to release more.

With this exercise, you are simulating anxiety by stirring your feelings when you think of something that makes you anxious. What's most important here is that you practice how to release anxiety <u>before</u> it happens. This way, you will be much more proficient at letting it go when it actually happens. It's just like practicing your lines to perform in a play or practicing a speech before you deliver it. Seeing it in your mind's eye or actually going through the motions of saying your lines or a speech in front of a mirror prepares your brain for the real event.

Your mind does not know the difference between real and imagined, especially if you really get into it. This is why you are able to simulate an anxious feeling with thought. Watching a movie is the same. Your subconscious mind does not know that what you are seeing is fantasy. For this reason, you either feel scared in a horror film or elevated in a movie that is motivational. You actually feel a rush when characters on the screen are experiencing success. It is a form of hypnosis as the images you see bypass your critical thinking with access to your subconscious. When you refocus your conscious mind, you tell yourself that what you are seeing is not real, yet have the ability to retain the feeling for a few hours after you've seen the movie. Unfortunately, the conscious mind will not accept that anxiety is an illusion until you reprogram your subconscious.

What if I don't feel anything? What if I can't let it go?
I have worked with people that say they have a hard time feeling anything. Most people do feel, but some don't at first. It's okay. We're all different. I'd say you need to sit with it longer and be patient. This is new territory, so to speak, for you as you've only learned to hold on to feelings. Most likely, no one has taught you that you have the natural-born ability to let go of these feelings at will. If you are having a hard time, be patient and notice even the subtlest of changes. Once you do, go through the process.

What do I do with this technique?
Great question! This technique is designed to help you practice letting go of anxiety. Its secondary function is to help program and retrain your mind to respond differently once anxiety actually hits. The more you practice this exercise, the better equipped you are to let go of anxiety when it bubbles up. When we want to reinforce an idea in hypnosis, we use a technique called compounding. This basically means that the more your subconscious mind hears an idea, the stronger it becomes on a subconscious level. It's the same as a commercial you see on tv, social media, YouTube, etc. The more often you see it, the more likely you are to act on purchasing the product or service. You are going to use compounding to retrain your less-than-conscious mind so it can respond more favorably to anxious feelings.

Secondly, you are going to use this technique to release any unfavorable feelings when they happen, and as soon as you feel them. Often times, the feeling starts off light and intensifies. Don't wait for it to intensify; start using the technique right away. This way, you can take control at the onset and not when it starts to run amok.

Releasing is an Innate Ability

Know that we release all the time without realizing it. When you've had a stressful day, you release it at the end. When you sigh, you release. As you lie down to fall asleep, hopefully you begin to release. When you know that there is a problem you can't quite tackle, you release by letting go or giving up. After you've solved a problem in life, you release. It's a natural ability but not done deliberately. Now you are going to do it consciously and intentionally.

I really hope that you are finding this information beneficial. Remember that the only way any of this is going to work for you is if you actually use it. If you don't use it, it won't do a thing, but if you do, I know you won't regret it. Let's dive into another technique you can use to temporarily eliminate anxiety almost instantly.

CHAPTER 11

Use Your Body to Rid Anxiety

∽

Until now, we've learned how to use our mind to release anxiety. Let's learn to use the body to do the same. No doubt that the mind is the most powerful way to release any negative feeling since this is where it stems from, but sometimes we need other means, and it's always good to have additional methods. The technique we're going to learn now may seem a bit unorthodox, but remember that if you are reading this book, you have to keep an open mind. No closed-mindedness with me, and you have to have fun.

When people experience regular anxiety, many of them freeze (called the freeze response). Think of when you have gotten frightened by something; you usually stop in your tracks. I imagine that since as humans, we are unsure of what to do for a moment when we are scared, stopping ourselves gives us the opportunity to focus, regroup and think about our next move. In contrast, anger creates movement and in many situations, retaliatory responses. In my opinion, anxiety creates this primal response because we are unclear as to why we feel anxious. We can have reasons for what we do, but are not completely sure, so we don't know how to respond. With anger, on the other hand, we know why we get angry, so we can either react or prepare a response. A few familiar examples are: someone cut you off on the road, your neighbor insulted you for the way you parked, your boss screamed at you for coming in late. These may create upset feelings or angry responses, especially if you feel you didn't deserve being treated this way, so you yell at the other driver, insult back, or somehow justify your behavior. The responses are quick and almost done without thinking.

Following, I would like to share with you a technique that you can use when starting to get anxious. Don't freeze. Instead, break the state, disengage. What does that mean? Do something that you wouldn't normally do when you get anxious. Sing, take a walk, run, do jumping jacks, call a friend, drum on the table, listen to music. Do anything in order to disengage the brain from the anxious pattern it is cycling through in order to create a new pattern. If you freeze, you make yourself feel vulnerable, not knowing what to do. Instead, tell your brain, we have to focus on something else that's not anxiety, and this is achieved by some form of physical activity. It breaks the anxious state and makes you switch to a more positive feeling because you separate your brain from the anxiety and move your body.

I love to watch how Cesar Milan (the famous "Dog Whisperer") trains dogs. When a dog initiates a crazy pattern like barking, growling, crazily jumping, biting its tail, etc., Cesar redirects them by pulling on their chain or tapping them with his fingers along with a "chiiiiit" sound. As soon as Cesar applies any of these techniques, the dog stops and disengages from the behavior. After doing this enough times, the dog's patterns break, and the behavior is automatically redirected. This "fixes" the dog's behavior in a relatively short period of time. There is no medication necessary, no dog psychologist, just good old-fashioned redirection. The same thing can be seen with children as parents instinctively adopt a similar behavior. How many times have we seen adults distract babies or small children when they cry? If you are a parent, you most likely did this yourself. Parents rattle something in front of their crying child, say "look, look over there!" They also say "I have something for you," or ask a random question. These are all ways of disengaging the brain from whatever the child is sad with to something that will either make them happy or distract them. It doesn't work all of the time, but often times it does. As adults, we revert to childhood and either become childish or childlike. We can use the same technique that Cesar Milan uses or that parents use on their children with success to redirect anxiety. It's not a fix-all, but it is in certain respects a temporary quick fix. We have to start retraining the brain to not get, or stay in, anxious states.

It's also important to keep in mind that when working with these feelings, your subconscious and brain have learned anxious responses to things that trigger it. First off, it's an illusion, a ghost, a phantasm. Next, feeling this way has become a learned pattern that is protecting you from something that you feel is a threat. You have to retrain your mind and brain in order to let it know that there is no threat. There is nothing harming you, and if there is, you would respond.

So you may think: isn't this a way of avoiding my anxiety? Isn't this suppression? It may seem that way, but it's different. Suppression is running away from the problem without wanting to acknowledge it. This is actively engaging in another activity with the intent of telling your brain to respond differently. It breaks the pattern while acknowledging the anxiety. Combined with the methods of release I just taught you, this goes well when used properly. The previous method is more passive; this is more active, but both can be a great benefit. Not everything works for everyone, however, and you have to use what works best for you. If either one has a better effect, then use that, or you can combine both. Your intention should always be to change the pattern so that you can develop a new learned response.

CHAPTER 12

Be Present for Peace

∽

I remember having said the following many times over in the time of the pandemic, "the present is a gift." Meaning that the present moment is a gift on its own. This play on words was well received with a deep truth by many when I released videos on relaxation and meditation in 2020. If you can achieve tapping into the present moment, it will give you an unmeasurable amount of peace, getting rid of any anxiety you may have. You should know, however, that gaining access to the present moment is easy and difficult at the same time.

It's easy to be present because all you have to do is become aware of something that captures your attention and continue to give that thing your full concentration. We do this all the time when we are really interested in something like a movie, when we study, or read something that we enjoy. Each individual brain predominantly processes information and gravitates toward either the visual, auditory, or kinesthetic (feelings) means. Which one depends on the person and what his or her brain prefers. If you are a visual person, some visual examples of things you can focus on are staring at the flickering flame of a candle, observing a painting, or looking at a spot on the wall. If you are more auditory inclined, you may focus on a sound like the humming of the air conditioner at home, sounds of the ocean, or the wind blowing, giving it your full attention. A feeling refers to directing your mind to a part of your body that feels some kind of pressure. For example, if you place your hand on your lap, direct your mind to your hand, and feel the pressure or weight that your hand exerts on your lap, feel how your foot rests on the ground, or how your arm rests on a lounge chair. These feelings of pressure on different parts of our body are usually ignored, but we can use them to our advantage by paying attention to them to become present.

Here's a little mind hack. Your mind cannot focus on two things at the same time, so instead of focusing on any anxious feelings, focus on something you see, hear, or feel. The mind has to choose one it cannot process both.

It's difficult to be present because our minds are constantly fleeting, looking for some kind of fulfillment, acceptance, or pleasure. The human mind has learned to multitask, which means that we do lots of things at once (great), but have a hard time focusing on just one (not so great). The irony is that we are all actually looking for what we already have...peace. Unfortunately, we don't believe we have it because it's just too easy to look inside. Our minds are way too active, we're super busy all the time, and can't seem to stop thinking. We have a hard time accepting that we can just let go of negative feelings and be internally stable, so we look outside of ourselves to find tranquility. We look for material things, the next new buzz, a better car, a remodeled room, a different look, clothes that are in fashion, the latest electronic gizmo, etcetera. Jumping and dancing from one thought to another makes it difficult to tame the mind and have it focus on just one thing, even for a few minutes. Our search leads us to happy moments when we obtain something new or different, but we are not really looking for happiness; we are unconsciously searching for peace. Happiness can change from one moment to the next; it's an illusion. True inner peace does not change; it's ever-present and real. Having a new car, gizmos, or gadgets is not bad; it just shouldn't be our main focus because we will never, ever find peace in acquiring new things. You know that, right? New things get old and they lose their excitement and value over time. We loooove our new car, but after some years, that love begins to fade, and we are out there looking for another new set of wheels. No matter how much we enjoy a new item, know that it's going to get old and diminish with time.

As the Oracle says in the movie Matrix Revolutions (the third one), "Everything that has a beginning has an end." Nothing can be further from the truth. All things physical obviously have a beginning, and because they are subject to the physical laws of this universe in one way or another, they must have an end. The same applies to us as human beings. As much as we try to prolong our existence on this Earth, we are just as subjected to universal laws as inanimate objects. Feelings have the same fate. Things that made you happy as a child no longer make you happy today. The very thing that upsets you today will change and no longer upset you later in life. Those foods that you don't like now can become a delicacy in your eyes as the years progress. You'll find yourself saying, " I used to hate spinach, broccoli, or Brussels sprouts as a child, but now I love them." (Not always; I still can't stand beets or Brussels sprouts.) Love has an end, and so does hate. It may take 1 year or 1,000, but with enough time, things are bound to change. The love for our loved ones changes sometimes for the better, and sometimes for the worse. "What about peace?" you may ask. There are nations that are at peace and then go to war. Didn't we say that peace is everlasting? Yes, but there is corrupted peace in the mind of the human being. True peace, and the not-fighting kind of peace, are not the same thing. Those at war did not have true peace to begin with. There was still a tinge of jealousy, hatred, lack of acceptance, or desire for what the other has. If that weren't the case, then why are they at war? Peace is undeniably the truest feeling one can have. You experience it in the womb, have it when you are a baby, and seek it for most of your life when you feel you have lost it.

I guarantee you this though: when you put forth the effort and focus on just one thing besides the thoughts your mind is conjuring, you will have access to the ever-present peace we've spoken about earlier in this book. Peace never dies; it never leaves us and is always inside of our very core. A true focus on something you can see, hear, or feel will give you an opening to the gateway of peace. You will also automatically blow the imaginary door in the center of your body wide open, allowing you to feel the peace that's always there and covered over by all of the excessive thinking we experience day by day. Any negative feelings will instantly dissolve, and they will flow through you without any effort at all. It's worth it to try even for just a little while.

This is the true power of becoming present. Why do we experience true peace when focusing on something other than ourselves? It is because we stop listening to the obsessive, and oppressive mind. The mind is a great tool which helps us get ahead and through life. When it runs rampant with uncontrolled thoughts, however, it becomes our adversary taking us out of the true inner peace we possess. It causes stress, anger, jealousy, fear, hatred, and a host of other negative feelings. The mind isn't bad; it's not the mind's fault. These are reactions we learn to survive and protect our physical body, reputation, feelings, loved ones, etc., from some real or imagined threat.

If you want to look further into this topic, I highly recommend "The Power of Now," a book by Eckhart Tolle. This book discusses the spiritual side of directing your focus to the present moment with part of the intent of easing anxiety and tension. It is a very powerful book that you can learn a lot from. When I read it I loved it and knew there was a deep truth and wisdom to it.

CHAPTER 13

Our Need to Create Problems

∾

Let's use the imagination again. I like to use the imagination, can you tell? I'd like you to imagine that right now you don't have any problems at all. Everything is taken care of, you don't have to worry about finances, your health is perfect, and everything you need is readily accessible without any effort. Most people would smile as I paint that scenario, but then their faces change, and many ask the question "What do I do?" In other words, what is my role in this life if everything I need is taken care of? Many would agree that although at first it sounds great and may even be great for a while, eventually, it will get quite boring. What do you think? Do you feel that life would be boring if all of your problems just went away and you didn't have to lift a finger so to speak to take care of anything? It depends on the problem, right? Think about it for a moment.

Here's what I've learned and observed for a bit more than half a century. We have the need to solve and sometimes create problems because it keeps us alive. Oh wow! What a bold statement, right? Well, there it is! Our ego, our mind, perhaps our identity has a need to live and survive as long as possible. Our ego has an obsessive need to make itself known and continue to carry out its existence for as much as it possibly can. The way that we exist is by solving problems in life. The famous philosopher Descartes said, "Cogito ergo sum." "I think, therefore I am." I like to look at this statement differently. (sorry Decartes) The philosophical statement establishes the certainty of one's existence by the act of thinking. I like to think of it in the reverse: "I am, therefore I think." In this way, we are looking at our thinking as part of our existence, not our existence tethered to our thinking.

We can stop thinking for a while and continue to exist. If we stopped thinking altogether, perhaps our ego or our identity would cease to exist, because who are we really? What makes us who we are? I know that Israel Maya, me, (and everyone else) is simply a compendium of thoughts that began to collect around 7 months of gestation. This is around the time hearing develops in the womb. All of the things my caretakers, elders, friends, and society taught me is what created who I am. Israel Maya is a character who accepted all of those ideas that he heard at a very young age and on a subconscious level continuing to reinforce them with his conscious mind. I've made tweaks along the way but the core ideas continue to be carried on by my thinking machine, the mind. If I stopped the constant thinking (which is very difficult to do) I wouldn't disappear I would continue to exist while redefining my character. In other words, I would no longer be subjected to all of the ideas I was inculcated with and have the ability to redefine who I am on my own terms. This is often referred to as an enlightened state of being. Without getting too much into it, part of being enlightened is the cessation of incessant thinking because we come to the realization, and acceptance that the mind is simply a tool, not who we are. We realize that the mind is behind the core of our problems. The mind does not like thought cessation because if we stop thinking, our ego panics and brings in a barrage of thoughts. Many of those thoughts are our problems and what we have to solve in our lives. Try it! See how long you can go without having any thoughts in your head. Ten seconds? Twenty? Even if you think to yourself, "Hey, I haven't thought anything in 10 seconds," it's too late; you're already thinking. The mind believes that it cannot be without thought as it ties its very existence to the function it does best: thinking. And the majority of thinking involves solving problems.

Now that we understand we create problems in order to solidify our existence, we have to be careful which problems we create. We can either create good problems or bad ones. Are there such things as good problems? I thought all problems were bad. Well, the word problem has a negative connotation, but it doesn't have to be a bad thing; it can also be good. Allow me to explain.

Bad problems are those difficulties in our lives that are unexpected, causing chaos, frustration, and relief only when the problem is solved. Those can be an indirect creation of our actions. They could be likened to self-sabotage. For example: driving while under the influence and getting caught. (Shouldn't do it even if one doesn't get caught.) The person that was DUI created the problem; it wasn't out of their control since they decided to drink and get behind the wheel of a car. Eating a food you know you are sensitive to or will make you sick. You ever hear some people say "I know this is going to make me sick but whatever," and then they eat it. Starting a fight with someone you know you can't win. All those are bad problems and ones that you choose to begin.

Good problems, on the other hand, are problems that we voluntarily create or volunteer ourselves to either help friends, acquaintances, or society to improve our lives or theirs. It's not a problem in the traditional sense, but it does require a solution. For example: when a friend asks us for help moving from one apartment to another, and we decide to lend a hand. This is a positive problem we've taken upon ourselves. If an institution you have ties to needs to raise funds and you agree to help, you've accepted upon yourself a positive problem. If you decide to open a center for abused individuals, this is a positive problem in which you help society.

So the question you should ask yourself is, are you creating good problems or bad problems? Often times, we don't realize that we are self-sabotaging (thus creating bad problems) until we see it ourselves, or it is brought to our awareness by others and we begin to realize... "Uh oh, I'm creating bad problems." If this is the case, it's time to change that and take action so that the difficulties in your life are positive ones as opposed to negative.

Questions to Ponder

- Is there any area of your life that you may be self-sabotaging by creating bad problems?
- Is there a reason or a need for this?
- If yes, is there anything you can do to stop it?
- What steps are you going to take to do so?
- Are you ready to begin creating good problems in your life?
- What steps will you take to start?

Anxiety is a Bad Problem
No kidding, right? Anxiety is a problem that our mind creates to self-sabotage. This is, of course, inadvertent; we don't do this knowingly, and please don't misunderstand me, I'm not blaming you for anything. Now that you know anxiety is an illusion, do you think it is easier to control? If you understand anxiety as a problem that the mind creates to keep you busy and continue its existence, can you see how the mere understanding causes you to gain some power and it to lose power?

I know that at the moment, this chapter is quite philosophical, but learning and knowing all you can about anxiety chips away at it so that you can understand it from a different perspective. Surely in the past you've lost fear of something by researching, understating, or experiencing it more. An example of this is when children (and sometimes adults) see a food they've never tried before and say they don't like it! You ask: "How do you know if you haven't tried it yet?" "I don't like it," they respond. It's the resistance of experiencing something new. Then sometimes they try it and they like it. The following is an experience from my own life as a teenager. I remember going to a place called 6 Flags Atlantis, a water theme park many years ago. There was a slide that went up about 150 feet high and was almost at a 90-degree angle. I was terrified of it but had to try it because all my friends were doing it. I was really nervous right up to the point where I was lying down with arms crossed on my chest on the slide. When the attendant pushed me down, it was a thrill and when I got to the bottom of the slide, I was ready to do it again. I remember going up and down that slide several times with confidence and wondering "Why did I fear it so much in the first place?" Other more adult examples are estate planning, paying taxes, finances, writing a will, and a doctor's visit. All of these have lessened anxiety when better understood. This is the way anxiety works. You fear certain things in your life because you don't understand them, but once you do, the fear loses its power over you and you gaining confidence and strength. Let's dive into how anxiety is attached to time.

CHAPTER 14

Anxiety, The Worry
of The Future

∾

If our mind focuses on painful things that happened in the past, it causes us to be sad, and we become depressed. If it focuses on possible future events, it gets agitated and becomes anxious.

- Depression equals the past.
- Anxiety equals the future.

It's what-if thinking. You don't get anxious about tense situations that have already happened, right? In other words, you don't get anxious about the big scary dog that growled at you yesterday. You may fear seeing it again in the future, or thinking what if I run into another scary dog? What do these things have in common with anxiety? They are a projection of the future, or what if thinking, so the anxiety is fear of a future occurrence. It's not fear of the past because you already know the outcome of a past event. You may also get anxious about things that happened in the past, which trigger a future event. As an example let's say you are constantly late to work. If your boss is strict on making sure employees arrive on time and you've already been reprimanded for tardiness, you may become anxious about the future. This is an anxiety rooted in past occurrences. In different scenarios, you may think "What if I lose my job?" "What if I said something offensive and my friend is mad at me?" "What if I'm sick and there's no cure?" We come up with "what-if" storylines all the time and drive ourselves crazy with them. Keep in mind that with everything we've already discussed, anxiety is also a focus on the future. This is another reason why it is an illusion. What you are worried about has not, and most likely will not ever happen. I bet that if you make a list of all the things you thought were going to happen, and when you reflect, cross out those that didn't happen, you'd eliminate most or all items of that list. I suggest you do that.

1. Make a list of all the bad things you thought might have happen in the past.
2. Reflect on if they happened or not.
3. Cross out those that didn't happen.
4. How many are you left with?

This is a solid way of seeing how unnecessary it was to worry so much, and honestly a waste of time. If you had a concern about something that needed a resolution and resolved it, then it was worth it, but if it never happened to begin with, then you wasted your precious time. This is time you could have spent doing something productive or enjoying life. Besides, unnecessary worry dumps adrenaline in the body, creates tension, affects the heart, and nervous system. Over time, it becomes very toxic. Is it worth it? Take a few moments to think about this and answer the question for yourself.

Live your life, don't die it.
We are all going to leave this earth one day; it's inevitable. Hopefully, we all live a long and healthy life. The question is how do you want to live the life that you've been given? Do you want to live your life, or do you want to die your life? Living your life means enjoying it, learning, laughing, having fun, and being productive. Dying your life means worrying, being miserable, and wasting time constantly believing something bad is going to happen. This is anxiety. It steals your thoughts, time,

happiness, and doesn't allow you to live your life; you die it slowly. It's a slow self-torture.

When you experience constant anxiety, you unconsciously shrink and take up less space, protecting and bracing yourself for what is to come. Perhaps what you worried about before may not have happened, but with anxiety, you may believe it's about to or is right around the corner. To understand how our bodies react to these stressful situations, think about getting angry for a moment. What do your hands do? Do they ball up into fists? How about if you hear something above you falling and it is inevitably going to hit you? Think about what happens to your neck, head, and back. You may bring your arms closer to your body, cause your neck to contract, and slightly arch your back in an attempt to make yourself smaller to avoid being hit. These are normal physical reactions that give us clues as to how our psyche functions when we feel threatened. When we feel this way and experience anxiety, we shrink physically and psychologically. We get smaller physically as a response to a perceived threat, psychologically because our thoughts become limited. You may not be aware of these reactions because they are unconscious, but think about them with curiosity, and you'll come to realize that most likely this is the case.

In complete contrast, when you feel safe, your very being expands, you take up more room, dream bigger, live larger, and enjoy your life more. Remember the release exercise we learned in chapter 10? When you opened the door, did you feel more expanded and as if your life force was flowing through you as opposed to being trapped inside? It's like a river flowing unimpeded by obstructions. Imagine with me now. Close your eyes and in your mind's eye, see a smooth, flowing river symbolic of your feelings. Hear the water rushing by as it speeds along the riverbank. Imagine opening the door we created before nice and wide to allow any feelings that are inside of you to flow like that river. If you let the feelings flow, you will experience an expansive feeling, allowing you to be more confident and grounded.

I remember thinking how much of an impact these ideas had on my life. It upset me to realize that the anxious thoughts I had were such a waste of time, and I finally came to the realization in my 30s that all of that time I spent worrying didn't amount to anything. It was simply a waste of time. I had an honest conversation with myself and asked, "Do you want to live your life or die it? I obviously chose to live it and have no regrets. You won't either. I'm not a big risk-taker, and I truly admire those people who are, but it doesn't mean that I don't take risks; I do. What I don't want for myself, though, is to be frozen, worrying about the decisions I make or want to make. I know people who take a long time deciding everything. They weigh every option and calculate every angle. I'm not saying that you should be careless in your decision-making, but don't torture yourself either with a constant back and forth saying "should I, or shouldn't I?" You know how anxiety works. It manifests in ways that cause you to worry about the decisions you make with second-guessing. Keep in mind that anxiety is a condition of the mind that focuses on what can go wrong in the future. If you feel you are taking way too long to make a decision on something, quicken the pace and make the decision. How does the saying go? "Piss or get off the pot." It's a grotesque expression and kind of funny, but it makes you think. C'mon, decide already. I reiterate, don't dive into a pool with no water saying "but it's a pool!" In contrast, don't make turtle-speed decisions either. We can't worry so much about the future. Think about your decisions and make them wisely because sometimes if you don't decide, life decides for you.

CHAPTER 15
What-if?

As human beings, our minds tend to play games. Games are fun, but some games are a bad idea. When it comes to anxiety, we usually play the what-if down game, which we spoke about earlier. What-if is the other side of the "worry about the future" coin. "What if something goes wrong?" "What if I don't make it this month in my finances?" "What if when I go out today, something bad happens?" This is the what-if down game. Really, there is no need to think this way. From what we learned in our last chapter, anxiety focuses on the future in a negative light. Do you want to win at that game? Play the what-if up game. What if everything goes well? What if great things happen today? What if I make more money this month than I've made in a long time?

Can we predict the future? Maybe in some things, sometimes, but most likely because we get lucky, not because we transcend time and see what's coming. There are times when experience whispers predictions in our ears. Usually, though, we just have to wait until something happens before we know what happened. So is it worth it to play the what-if down game? I think you know the answer to that. It's a waste of time and not worth it. It's just massaging anxiety. Again, as previously mentioned, you don't have to take non-calculated risks. Calculate your risks, make sure you make proper decisions, and don't constantly second-guess your every move. Making mistakes is part of living and learning, so if you made an error because of a miscalculation, know that this is part of life and that everyone makes mistakes. You may make difficult financial mistakes, mistakes in relationships, or with your health, but again, it's part of living. No one welcomes mistakes, but when they happen, do your best to get to the other side when you realize the right decision wasn't made.

One time I made a quick decision on a small real estate investment of $70,000 by borrowing the money against my house. You'll see why I said small in a minute. It was a time when flipping pre-construction prices was popular and profitable for many. I took a risk but took it as the market began to slow down. I decided on one property for $35,000, and when a friend of mine said he'd jump in with me, I took another for a total of $70K. After two months, my friend bailed on me, and I was left making the payments for both properties. A short time after, the real estate bubble burst, and I was forced to either purchase the properties at $350,000 each or walk away from them. I tried getting a loan and was about to be approved, making me fall into a $700,000 debt. You understand now why $70K was small? I decided to dump both properties and lose the $70K. I went from lawyer to lawyer to see if I could get out of the contract and recuperate my money. In the meantime, my cousin, an amazing lawyer (who I feel indebted to forever), found a tiny clause in a huge contract. The clause stated that if the property I purchased was completely built by a certain date, I was bound to the contract and had to purchase the property. If the finish date exceeded that stated on the contract, the money was to be returned to me with interest.

I waited with great anticipation, calling the builder's office every few weeks to see if the place had been completed. I had lots of anxiety, and played a lot of the what-if down game back then.

Sleepless nights became part of a routine, and swirling thoughts of what would happen if I had acquire this debt consumed me. This was before I knew any of these techniques, ha. As it turned out, one of the properties was completed before the specified date, but the second was not. Whew! My genius lawyer cousin then drafted a letter sending it to the builder.

After having to sign a non-disclosure agreement, $38,000 was returned to me. I paid off the loan with that money and had also been making payments beforehand, so when I submitted my payment to the mortgage company, I was at $0 debt. Unfortunately, in the process, I lost $50,000, but it became a learning experience for me. Sometimes we win, and sometimes we lose. In this case I lost but reduced my fear of investing. Today I invest, and weigh the risks but don't jump into something that I don't research enough, not excessively, just enough to make an informed decision. Once I decide yes I go forward and don't worry about it. If I win, great, and if I lose, I know it's part of the risk. I like winning, though.

CHAPTER 16

Let it Go or Let it Happen

∾

Providing that we have a relatively normal upbringing, one of the worst experiences we can have at any given moment in our lives is a panic attack. It's frightening, debilitating, makes you feel extremely vulnerable, and you truly believe you are going to die. That's why so many people who have panic attacks go to the emergency room. I can remember my first panic attack. It was horrible. I paced the floor back and forth, wondering what was going on and why I felt so bad. My heart raced as if I was running a marathon, my breath quickened, I felt jittery, and wanted to jump out of my skin. At that moment, I just wanted the feeling to go away. I'd do anything if I could only get rid of it. Every time I felt it coming on, I would jump out of my chair, start pacing, and say to myself, "Oh no! Here it comes again." The feeling I had was: wanting to die to stop the panic, and of course, not wanting to die at the same time because I value life. It totally messes with your brain.

The most common response is to somehow try to suppress the panicky feelings that come up. At least, at the beginning, this is how I approached it, and I'm sure a large portion of the 36.4 million people that have panic attacks on a yearly basis do as well. When I became more aware of anxiety, what it is, and how to deal with it, I came to a realization, an epitome of some sort. I asked myself (I like to ask a lot of questions), "What if I just let the panic attack happen?" What if I don't suppress it and take a BRING IT ON attitude? What would happen then? Would I really die like I think I'm going to?" So I did just that. Instead of trying to suppress the feelings of anxiety, I told myself "I'm letting anxiety take over my whole body without me doing anything about it." It was a scary decision because no one wants to die from anxiety, but what happened was just the opposite. I started to laugh since I felt I was controlling the feelings as opposed to the opposite being true. Besides being a relief, it was a real breakthrough, so I've taught my clients the same thing. When you are having anxiety or panic, don't resist it. Imagine that the feeling is completely taking over your body and let happen what is supposed to happen, even if you were to die. If you've had enough panic attacks to know even a little about them, you've already come to the conclusion that a panic attack will not kill you despite the feelings. A pounding heart in even a relatively healthy individual can definitely take it. You may pass out from hyperventilating, but that's only because you are blowing off too much CO_2. It's totally controllable if you slow down your breathing, or blow into a paper bag ha ha.

I realize that letting happen to you the very same thing that you want to avoid seems counterproductive, and that's exactly why I waited so long before mentioning it. It may seem scary to do this. What's the worst that can happen? As we've already stated before, you are not going to die from it, and you will discover that the feeling of panic passes quicker than if you were suppressing it. Most likely you are not experiencing a panic attack right now, so you can't fully do what I've just discussed at the moment, but it doesn't hurt to try. Below we will do just that in a simulation exercise. In order for this to be more effective you may have to wait until it comes on for real, but at the very least, you now have a way of instantly dealing with it. That again puts you in charge of what you are feeling. Remember that every technique and method we do here is in light of putting you in charge and taking control of your emotions. Your responsibility is to be disciplined, practice, and take charge.

I know I mentioned above that you would have to wait until an attack hits to do this, but maybe you don't. What if you imagined yourself having a panic attack right now? If you feel brave enough do the following exercise. If not, then feel free to skip it and come back to it at a later time or use it when you actually feel anxious.

Close your eyes and imagine what it feels like to have the jitters from panic? What if you summoned the very feelings you are trying to avoid and begin to focus on them....the pounding heart, fast-paced breathing, wanting to run away or jump out of your skin, and all of the feelings that accompany panic attacks? You can also focus on something that makes you feel anxious. When you feel the feelings, tell yourself "I'm going to let anxiety completely take over my body." Sit quietly and allow the feelings to come up and flow through you without any resistance. In this way, you are removing fear associated with panic and allowing yourself to take control of the fear. This happens quite often; people fear the panic, not knowing when it's going to strike. Trust in the process, my friend. Below, I enumerate what I've discussed above so it's easier to follow:

1. Sit quietly
2. Focus on what a panic attack is and how you feel when it happens, imagine a time when it actually happened, or something that makes you feel anxious.
3. If the feelings come up, tell yourself you are going to let it take over you without any resistance.
4. Close your eyes and let the feelings flow through you, no matter how scary it may be.

You may also incorporate the technique where you place an opening in the center of your body, since this is where feelings come up. Once you feel those feelings, though, don't resist them.

Let them flow through you. When you are finished, evaluate how you feel. If you were apprehensive about doing this at first ask yourself: Is it as bad as I thought it would be? Do you feel that you have more of an ability to take charge of anxiety now that you know you can actually control it and let it go? This chapter is similar to the release technique we learned in chapter 10, but here we are more focused on letting go of a panic attack, which is much more intense. Actually, if I were to sum up this work in a few words, it would be:

Be aware and let it go.

Letting the feelings take over you without resistance is a way of letting them go. The process is active and passive at the same time. This may sound like I'm joking, but you are actively being passive. Active for taking the steps to opening up to the feelings, and passive as you allow them to leave without any obstruction. Having awareness and letting things go teaches you everything you need to have complete freedom from anxiety. All else is just an explanation or commentary. Most of the time, we are not aware of our feelings because we've gotten so used to them. At some point, anxiety becomes a learned response, as we spoke about before, and we may not notice that it's brewing within us since we're distracted from it until it intensifies. The anxiety is there at a low level, but we chose to ignore it with our ability to select what we feel.

When I began to have anxiety in the late 1990s, the internet was just beginning to gain popularity. Imagine that: the internet was being born, and I was there to witness it. We used to say www dot before a website. My point is that there are a lot more distractions today than there were back then. Now you can download an app for practically anything, and distractions are easy to have. When this was starting for me, you couldn't get movies online, and Netflix wasn't even a thing yet. You still had to go to Blockbuster Video (a physical store) to rent a movie for a few days and bring it back. Today, you don't have to worry about watching a movie, finding a show, or starting a new series with so many websites and apps available, many of which you get for free with subscriptions or memberships to something. You also have YouTube, and social media for free, which can keep you occupied for hours at a time with practically any topic.

With so many distractions available, it's easy to pull our attention away from what is really happening inside of us. When we pay close attention, there it is. You may have a low level of anxiety, which you feel or even begins to intensify if you focus on it. Well, the best thing you can do for yourself is to be aware of your feelings and let negative ones go with the method I taught you earlier. Giving those feelings an outlet is the best gift you can give yourself. Negative feelings are the storm that you experience superimposed on the peace that's always there. The peace is a friend who never leaves. If you are aware of everything I mention here, you will notice that as you let go of unwanted feelings, you begin to instantly feel a small level of peace, which then grows. You don't need to do anything in order to have it; it's right there, always waiting for you. Take time to become aware of what feelings you have in the center of your body and let them go.

CHAPTER 17

Open the Door, Slam it Shut!

∾

Throughout this work, you've learned to use your imagination in an advantageous way. Since your imagination creates anxiety (an illusion), you can also use that same imagination to combat anxiety as well. We created an opening in the center part of your body that is now used to allow feelings to flow through you instead of getting stuck inside. As you already know, stuck feelings cause a vicious cycle of more internal pressure, making you feel worse. The worse you feel, the more feelings come up and get trapped, creating an unending hamster wheel of anxiety. As I mentioned before, every technique and exercise in this book is designed to empower you so that you can come to the same realization I did, which is "This isn't as bad as I thought it was." Without invalidating your feelings, I know it feels horrible, but when you take control, nothing is as bad as you thought it was because you develop a sense of confidence, helping you stand taller and prouder. If you have been following my suggestions up to this point, you should feel proud of yourself for actively doing something to counteract a feeling that many people fall prey to, not knowing what to do. You now have an edge that puts you way ahead of many who are not aware. Awareness is the key to letting go of anything you don't want in your life. If you don't know what's going on inside of you and you have no idea of how to fix it, then you never will. It's just that simple, so now I'm going to give you another exercise that will help you understand letting go at an even deeper level. This next part was a real eye-opener for me, and I hope it will be for you as well.

Open the Door / Slam it Shut

By now you have no doubt felt the benefits of the peace that's instantly felt when you let feelings flow through you with the open door in your body's center part. The ultimate goal is to allow the opening you created to stay open as much as possible so that nothing ever bothers you. If you've noticed, that opening ends up closing on its own. For the most part, when working with the opening, we don't will or want it to close; it just happens, and we are left with a closed door that we then have to reopen when it comes to our awareness. What if you slammed the door shut, though? Seriously. What if you willfully opened the door, let the feelings flow through you, and then slammed that door shut? Let's try it together and see how it feels. The reason we are doing this is to have a stark contrast so that we come to a true realization of its benefits. Here we go.

1. Sit quietly in a place where you won't be disturbed.
2. Bring your attention to your feeling center (stomach, chest, or both).
3. Give that area an opening with your imagination.
4. Allow all feelings to flow through you.
5. Slam the door shut for a few moments and compare the two.
6. Reopen the door and leave it open.

I clearly remember the first time I did this, and it was a real eye-opener, bringing me awareness to three things. First was to realize how unaware I was about a tightly shut door, so in this case I didn't know that I didn't know. Second was the level of control I have over my feelings. Third was (once you become aware) how terrible it feels to slam the door and arrest the beautiful flow of all emotions.

Questions to Ponder

- What did you feel?
- Have you come to an awareness that you can have control over your emotions?
- Does an exercise like this change the way you view holding on to anxiety or any negative feelings?
- What can you do to improve your emotional situation?

I am aware that it takes effort to keep that door open, but at one time in our lives, feelings flowed through us effortlessly, and the door was always open, so to speak. Observe children, or think of ones you've interacted with. When they get upset, it happens in the moment. After a little while passes, they are back to their same selves without any remorse. In fact, if they've misbehaved and were punished, they'll sometimes go right back to doing the same thing they were punished for without skipping a beat. They don't think of the consequences, mostly because children don't have impulse control, but they have memory. They just don't hold on to feelings like adults do. That is the key! They don't hold on to feelings; we do. If you are a parent, aunt, or uncle, haven't you ever gotten upset at your child, or one for doing something they shouldn't be doing, then disciplined them, and later you think they are still upset with you, but they aren't? When you interact with them, it's like nothing ever happened. Did you ever think "I wish I could do that." Part of why they let go is their innocence, and the other part is that they haven't experienced keeping the door closed. It's open all the time. This says to us that we have that same ability to let go of things that bother us since we were already born with it; we just need to be willing.

I am also aware that we may not be able to keep that door open when we are living our busy lives because the door automatically shuts when we stop paying attention to it. We can, however, develop a habit of opening it and letting go of unwanted feelings when they arise. I tell you all of this so that you don't think that you are doing something wrong if you can't keep that door open all the time. Don't worry, you're okay. This is a learning process, and as long as you are engaged in doing something about negative feelings that come up, you are way ahead of the game.

CHAPTER 18

Negative Self-Talk

∾

As previously mentioned, our minds are always spinning their wheels. We have constant self-talk going on in our heads so much so that at times we don't even notice it; it's almost like background noise. I would even say that it has probably become comforting to some extent when the mind goes on endless monologues. I don't know if that is the way it's supposed to be since we often times repeat loops of ideas in our minds over and over again. We may get a song stuck in our heads repeating the same lines, judge ourselves and others, and even have direct conversations with other people on what we want to tell them. The mind is supposed to be a tool, not be all-consuming. Nonetheless, with all the ideas running rampant in our heads, we have to be careful with the type of talk we are giving ourselves. Here again is where we must have self-awareness on what we are thinking because while positive self-talk is always a good thing, negative self-talk is destructive.

When anxiety becomes a part of our lives, we often engage in negative self-talk that leads our minds astray. This negative self-talk inevitably results in harsh judgments of ourselves and others. It will also lead to nervous thoughts that could inevitably bring us to more anxiety. To avoid this, we must be aware of what we are thinking for some time until we retrain our mind to think more positively. If you find yourself having anxious thoughts, gently steer your thoughts away to something more positive. As you have already experienced in life, I'm sure, the firmer you are with your mind, the less it cooperates with you, so that's why the best tactic is to be gentle with it. Do I have to bring up the pink elephant in the room example? I guess I just did. Tell yourself that you would rather think about something more positive and that it's better for you overall. Some people (I'm not saying you) identify themselves with constant negative thinking. They even subconsciously enjoy the drama that is involved in it, so if you have a tinge of that (not saying you do, but if) then your best bet is to change the way you think. Is it easy? Well, yes and no. All you have to do is change the way you think. That's easy, isn't it? That's the yes part. The no part is that habits are difficult to break, especially when you are using the conscious mind or willpower.

Willpower

It has a great ring to it, doesn't it? Both words have strength in them, especially power. Willpower is a great way to give yourself a boost when you are making a temporary change or doing something competitive. It is temporary because willpower itself resides in the conscious mind, not having enough of an effect on the subconscious mind to make permanent changes. As we mentioned before, the subconscious is where our identity lies. It's the place of our mind that absorbed all of the ideas our caretakers and friends planted within us when we were children. We became the people we are based upon what we've learned, so making changes involves working with our own subconscious programming. Think of dieting, stopping to smoke, not having that extra piece of cake, cutting down on coffee, or any behavior which isn't productive. With the positive or negative repetition of an action, we achieve automated subconscious programming since we no longer have to think about those behaviors in the future. It actually makes our lives easier when we do them without too much thought, like driving, shaving, brushing our teeth, tying our shoes, or anything that becomes automatic. Those behaviors become automatic and reside in the subconscious part of the mind.

As much as we try to will it away, the behavior change is usually short-lived. The reason for this is that there is unconscious resistance to make a change to something we've already accepted on a subconscious level. This resistance is why we can't force our minds to just stop thinking negative thoughts. Willpower against negative thinking may work temporarily, but it returns and sometimes with a vengeance. We must be less threatening with the subconscious in order to have a more positive effect on it. There is a more effective way to make subconscious changes. One of them we have already discussed, which is hypnosis. The other is self-hypnosis. In our next chapter, I will teach you the basics of how to self-hypnotize. Don't worry, you can't get stuck in hypnosis forever, but it can have a strong effect on making changes in your life because now you are able to work directly with the part of you that has subconscious programming.

CHAPTER 19

Learning Self-Hypnosis

In this next section, I present to you a different form of empowerment in order to let go of negative thoughts and feelings. The goal, as mentioned in the previous chapter, is to affect the subconscious part of you so that you can change the programming in it. Keep in mind that we are already programmed to react or respond in negative ways from our earlier years. The work that we are doing in this book and in the following section aims at deprogramming negative thought patterns like anxiety so that you can have the freedom you are looking for. Every bit of understanding, application of exercises given, challenge of beliefs, and practice of what you've learned brings you closer to achieving your goal, allowing you to live the life you deserve. The aforementioned is a powerful holistic approach to conquering anxiety from many different angles. It is very different than just taking a pill to cover up any symptoms. The use and application of self-hypnosis gives you an additional tool you can apply to rid yourself of anxiety. Below I teach you a simple version of self-hypnosis as there is more, but it's the best we can do through a book. Buckle up. This next part is pretty intense. There's a lot to take in but definitely worth it as it can make a big impact on your self-growth.

What is self-hypnosis?
Self-hypnosis is a way of putting yourself into a deeply relaxed state of mind, so that you can have access to the subconscious part of your mind. Since the conscious part of the mind is very active, it overpowers subconscious thoughts in a way that you are not aware of them. When the mind calms, it is easier to be

in touch and work with the subconscious while the mental noise is tamed.

Bypassing the protective factor of the subconscious.
In hypnotherapy, the protective factor that aids in blocking thoughts, ideas, and suggestions from entering the subconscious is called the critical factor. The job of the critical factor is a very important one because it shields our identity from radical change. An identity that is intact is important in our lives since it defines who we are, albeit our identity is a compendium of the collected ideas of our past and what we are taught. Nonetheless, if we wish to be part of society with a stable identity, we must have something that protects those subconscious ideas; this is the critical factor. As we mentioned before, if I tell you something that is in direct conflict with your subconscious belief, your critical factor causes the idea to be rejected. For example: if I show you a circle and tell you it's a square, your automatic response without thinking about it is to immediately reject what I said, causing you to say "no, it's not; it's a circle!" By the time we are three or four years of age, we develop a critical factor around many ideas as our identity forms, and we strive to create a persona. I've randomly asked children of this age things that would conflict with already established beliefs like shapes and colors just to see what they would say. The result is an immediate rejection and resistance. It's fascinating to watch as I have instant confirmation that as children we have the ability to protect what we learn. The critical factor is intact and doing its job properly, so this works in the child's and our favor. It becomes counterproductive when we learn and establish subconscious ideas that are harmful, which the critical factor then protects, thereby making them more difficult to eliminate or replace later in life. For example, if a child was told "You're no good," "You're just a bad kid," "You will never amount to anything in life," or here's a classic "you're going to me a loser just like me." These ideas bring destructive

thoughts with serious consequences, and often times are a projection of the one who is saying it.

When it comes to anxiety, if we see our caretakers reacting in constant fear, or we take on beliefs that are fearful in nature either based on things that we see or hear, it becomes instilled in us, creating a fearful personality. In other words, the fear that we learn makes us fearful in life, with a critical factor that protects fear-based reactions and ways of living. The establishment of these reactions doesn't have to only occur in childhood; it can also happen in the teenage or adult years if an event is powerful enough to make you change. For example, if you have an embarrassing experience on stage, you may think to yourself, "I'm never getting up on stage again." This can severely impair your ability to do any kind of acting or public speaking in the future. I know people that have mild to severe panic attacks when they have to do public speaking for work, and this is because they accepted some belief in their subconscious that says they are no good at it. This is another illusion since public speaking is a skill set that you can learn. Some people are better than others depending upon how much work they put into it, and their character traits but take it from me who used to be terrified of public speaking and now does it with ease in front of any number of people: anyone can do it once they learn how. The amount of people is just a number. If you do it in front of 10, you can do it in front of 1,000.

To reiterate my point, once you bypass your own critical factor with the establishment of any idea, your critical factor will protect that idea, making changes more difficult and seemingly impossible. Hypnosis and self-hypnosis help you bypass your own critical factor to understand and release rooted ideas in the subconscious in order to create positive change.

It's easier than you think.
The critical factor is a guard (so to speak) who protects the opening of the subconscious door, letting through only those ideas that are in congruence with what you have been programmed, all the while rejecting those that are in conflict. Based on previous discussions, it may seem as if bypassing that resistance is very difficult, but it's easier than you think when, and if, you know how. You see, the critical factor is based upon logical thinking. It resides in the conscious part of your mind, which is basically logical. However, when you do, say, or hear something that you don't fully understand, it throws off the critical factor, leaving it temporarily suspended with access to the subconscious. We can all relate to the following really cool example. You see a movie, and either while you are watching it, or by the end of the movie, you feel like the character or are inspired by them. Why? Why do movies make us, and I repeat MAKE US, feel this way? I'll tell you why. When you see something on screen that you know is impossible, like a person flying, for example. You know it's not real because humans can't fly, as your critical factor tells you. (That's not an illusion.) Yet, you are actually seeing someone fly, so this confuses the critical factor because although it's impossible, you are still seeing it. When this happens, the critical factor is displaced, suspended, and the images you are seeing on the screen enter your subconscious mind, creating a connection to you with the flying character, hero, etcetera. This will give you a temporary lift (pun) as you imagine yourself flying or doing the amazing things you are seeing in the movie. You literally believe you can do what you are seeing and replay it in your mind (especially when you are a child) as if it's you. If you don't resonate with flying, then pick something you do resonate with, like a great public speaker, a person that made a difference in the world, a karate expert, etcetera. This person becomes you, and you become inspired by what you see. You, my friend, have been hypnotized. Yes, that's the way hypnosis works. As balanced adults, however, we come to the eventual realization

that the extraordinary things we see on screen are produced in a studio with a controlled and scripted environment, either green-screened, CGI (computer-generated imagery), or AI-generated. This realization prevents us from jumping off a building to test our flying skills or doesn't make us put radioactive spiders on our arms so that we can spin webs (Spiderman). Some unfortunate souls are not as lucky, though, as there are plenty of adults that believe they can do many of the stunts they see on screen and get hurt or end up dying. Just look on social media. Not to mention children that have tried to jump out of a window thinking they can fly like Superman— very sad.

Music also has a similar hypnotic effect that movies do, in an auditory way as opposed to visual. Feeling a lift from music that resonates with you either because it's something that you want to achieve or a similar scenario of your life described in the song (like a breakup or self-empowerment) is a simple conscious mind critical factor bypass with the establishment of temporary suggestions in the subconscious. Songs bypass our critical factor and cause its displacement because the conscious mind relaxes when it listens to music. This is especially true if you resonate with the music, the singer, or the message because you trust either one or all. Think of those songs that have made an incredible impact on our society. The songs themselves are hypnotic, with words that are powerful and moving, for example: "I will survive," "Don't stop believing," "You gave love a bad name," "I'm a survivor." If you listen or have listened to pop culture music, then surely you would have felt this way in the past.

Why temporary and not permanent?

With a song or movie, if we bypass the critical factor and gain access to the subconscious mind, why don't the suggestions we hear cause permanent changes within us? It is because a song is not enough to cause this type of change. As complicated humans, we sometimes require a deeper understanding of why we act the way we do in order to let things go. We like to do therapy and dig into the different psychological layers, but if we would take a simpler approach, we'd let things go a lot faster when we realize that the thoughts we so dearly hold on to are betraying us. In addition, listening to a song only has a temporary effect because we are missing the compounding component we spoke about way back in chapter 9. Compounding is the repetition of an idea in the subconscious, which makes it stronger as it gets repeated. This is how we learn and establish ideas as children. Ideas are repeated over and over again when we hear them from our caretakers or see a visual representation of something we establish as a belief. A song is four minutes long at most, and we are not in a bypassed critical factor state the whole time while listening to music, as distractions are always an issue. When we hear the song again, we've already re-solidified ideas that don't serve us, washing away the message we heard from the song. The length of the song is not enough time to reprogram old habits. Some people have incredible breakthroughs within a short amount of time, so the realization with a song or deciding to make a change from destructive behavior with enough conviction can cause a strong shift. It's not the norm, but it can happen.

Start with, and state your intentions.

Intentions are a powerful way to move your mind in the direction you want it to go. Often times, we are more creative than we give ourselves credit for; if we have a strong self-belief, we discover our creativity and hidden talents.

Intentions are driving forces and a request for help from your unconscious thinking as you cause it to focus on what your needs are. I use intentions all the time, especially when I write or get blocked. I tell myself, "I'm now going to come up with creative ideas to express this or that." "I am going to write an amazing piece about _____." It's not magic, but it is magical in the sense that your mind focuses on what you need creating easier success. This is an additional tool that you can use to your advantage in order to focus your mind.

How to bypass your own critical factor
Believe it or not, your critical factor has already been bypassed by reading this book. Actually, any book will do as long as it's interesting material that you resonate with. If not, you'll reject the incoming ideas, but if you listen to or read ideas with an open mind and are challenged by them, your critical factor will be suspended, and you gain access to the subconscious mind. This happens on a less-than-conscious level with minimal conscious understanding. Haven't you ever heard of someone, or maybe have said yourself "Such and such book, seminar, workshop, session changed my life?" None of those things can change your life; it's the ideas and the acceptance of them that create a change. Nonetheless, here is the crux of why we have explained so much. The way you bypass your own critical factor is by telling yourself something you know you can definitely do and then by telling yourself you can't do it. Don't worry, I'll explain what that means. Also, when you are ready to come out of the hypnotic state, I use the phrase "break the state." This means to take yourself out of the relaxed state in order to transition to a more "alert" state. It's done with an intention of breaking that state as you say (or think to yourself) "I'm now coming out of the relaxed state on the count of three," and then count to three opening your eyes.

Here are those steps enumerated. Read them first and practice sitting in a space where you won't be interrupted for a few minutes:

1. Place your hands on your laps. (Laps is correct, I looked it up. lol)
2. Close your eyes and tell yourself that you are going to relax your arms/hands to the point that they don't work.
3. When you have them that relaxed, try and lift either your right or left arm.
4. When you are ready, break the state and open your eyes.

Were you able to lift the arm? The idea was to relax both arms to the point where they don't work. You may say: "But I can always lift my arm!" This is true, but what if you relaxed them so deeply that you couldn't?

With the above exercise, one of two things happened: either you lifted your arm because you told yourself "I can still lift my arm," thereby <u>not</u> bypassing the critical factor (this isn't what we want), or your arm stayed put feeling heavy (in which case you bypassed your critical factor). The idea is to convince yourself (or fake yourself out) that you can relax your arm to such an extent that it doesn't move when you try to lift it. This is possible. When it doesn't move, your critical factor won't understand what is happening since you are always able to move your body at will. This causes a temporary displacement of the critical factor, giving you an open door to the subconscious mind. At this point, you will have to act fast, taking the necessary steps that I will teach you to enter the somnambulistic or hypnotic state. That's the concept. It's simple, and maybe even so simple that some may reject the idea that it can actually do anything, but trust me, the more you understand, the more sense it makes.

If your mind is still curious, wondering about the veracity of such a claim, I invite you to look up a gentleman named Dave Elman who developed these techniques. Dave Elman was one of the best hypnotists in his time, living from 1900-1967. As a young boy, he was fascinated with hypnosis and figured out a way to hypnotize people in record time as opposed to his peer adult hypnotists. He understood the bypass of the conscious mind's critical factor, and when he got older, traveled the US for many years teaching dentists, surgeons, dermatologists, and other doctors how to hypnotize their patients for mental pain control. Dave Elman's classes and teachings were an absolute success and worked beautifully for the physicians who used his methods. If you want to dig even deeper, look up the name Dr. James Esdaile, a surgeon who operated on people using hypnotic trances alone. When I say operated, I mean cutting out large tumors and performing amputations with the patients experiencing no pain and a quicker recovery time in an era where neither ether nor anesthetics existed. Dr. Esdaile lived in the 1800s and didn't understand hypnosis as well as Dave Elman, who was not a doctor. (He says that over and over again in his book and course.) In fact, the hypnotic induction "The Elman Induction" was named after him because he created it, helping patients achieve hypnosis within 1-3 minutes as opposed to hours with others. At the time of this writing, you can find the entire live course Dave Elman gave to medical doctors on YouTube. He also wrote a book named Hypnotherapy, which is out of print but based upon the classes he gave to those medical doctors. His book and audio course go over the critical factor and how to utilize hypnosis extensively with many examples.

For me, this is an exciting topic to write about because Dave Elman was a master at hypnotizing people, achieving mental anesthesia, and finding people's childhood traumas to help them let go. He helped thousands. When I became a hypnotherapist, I learned with someone who was very well versed in Elman techniques, but it's even better when you learn from the master himself, although I never met him other than through his book and audio course. After studying and using his methods, my patients had tremendous success with letting go of childhood traumas, fears, anxieties, and addictions. I mention Elman and Esdaile here in case you get serious about self-hypnosis and would like to go beyond the scope of this work.

I know how to bypass my own critical factor. Now what?
Now that you understand how to bypass the critical factor, it's time for you to learn the next step: deepening the state. Bypassing the critical factor alone is still not enough. You need to deepen the state in order for you to stay in a hypnotic state, and that is achieved by a deepening technique I will teach you. When learning how to bypass the critical factor, I asked you to try and lift your arm. In hypnosis, we use the eyelid muscles because they are the first and easiest to relax. Closing the eyes is not only easy but it feels good as well, so for now, we are going to use the eyelids in order to bypass the critical factor. You can then switch to another body part later on if you want like an arm or leg.

I'm going to explain the whole thing here first, then we will enumerate. To recap, when you want to self-hypnotize, find a quiet space where you won't be disturbed. Keep your phone and devices on mute so they don't interrupt your relaxation. You are going to shift your eyes upward, hold them there, and when you are ready, give yourself the command "relax" out loud. Once you say that word, instantly close your eyes. This will be your trigger word to go into a self-hypnotic state. Then tell yourself that your eyes are so relaxed you can't open them no matter how hard you try, and with that same desire to want them <u>not to open,</u> test them. Once you've tested them and they don't open, stop testing and tell yourself that in a moment you are going to open and close your eyes, and when you close them, you will relax your body and mind 10 times deeper. This is the deepening technique I wrote about earlier. Then open and close your eyes, letting yourself relax 10x deeper. Give yourself a few moments and tell yourself that you are now going to open and close your eyes a second time, but this time you will double your relaxation. Open and close, doubling your relaxation. Then do a third time, doubling your relaxation again. After achieving this, check yourself and notice how relaxed you are. At this point, if you feel calm and in a deepened state of relaxation, give yourself suggestions. We will go over those soon. For now, I want you to understand the concept of self-hypnosis and how to get there.

The Process

1. Get comfortable. Shift your eyes upward with the intention of entering a deeply relaxed state of mind and hold them there for a few moments.
2. Command your body with the trigger word "relax."
3. Allow your eyes to instantly close without any hesitation.
4. Tell yourself that your eyes are so relaxed you are not able to open them.
5. When they are that relaxed, test them and when they can't open, stop testing.
6. Tell yourself that you are now removing the relaxation temporarily so that you can open and close your eyes, but when they close, your body and mind will relax 10 times deeper, then follow through.
7. Tell yourself you are going to open and close a second time, but double your relaxation once your eyes close.
8. Open and close your eyes a third time, doubling your relaxation once again.
9. Give yourself suggestions.
10. When you are ready to come out of the self-hypnotized state, tell yourself "I'm now coming out of the hypnotic state at the count of 3. One....Two...Three...and open your eyes, breaking the state."

This is basically how it works. It seems like a lot of steps, but it gets easier once you familiarize yourself with them. Plus, you don't have to learn how to open and close your eyes; you've been doing that all your life. It's when to do each thing that takes a little practice, but trust me, it's not hard. Once you understand the mechanics of self-hypnosis, you have to know what to tell yourself after achieving the relaxed mental state.

What suggestions do I give my subconscious?

The easy answer is positive ones. That is obvious, but how to word them is important. We want to use a positive approach as opposed to a negatively worded one. If you've ever worked with affirmations, it's the same rule of thumb.

- Instead of: "don't be worried," it's better to say "be calm."
- Instead of: "I won't be nervous," say, "I remain relaxed."
- Instead of: "I don't feel any stress," say "my body and mind feel a sense of peace."

In this way, we have a positive approach as opposed to a negatively steered one. Why? The subconscious mind does not understand "don't." Don't think of a chair right now! How do you do that? You think of a chair and then remove it. How do we not be anxious? We first have to imagine anxious and then remove it from our minds, thereby affirming it. Our minds have a hard time understanding things that lack existence because for us, everything that we interact with exists. For this reason, children many times do the exact opposite of when we tell them DON'T do this. "Don't cross the street by yourself!" It's better to say: "Only cross the street with an adult; it's safer." Their mind doesn't understand the don't part. When you are in the hypnotic, relaxed state of mind, you will then need to give yourself suggestions to release and counteract anxiety, which we will cover shortly.

Begin with this: I release any and all experiences that may have caused anxiety in the past or could cause in the future, whether I remember them or not.

You may, of course, create your own variation of this suggestion. It is designed to counteract a life event that may have created anxiety in the first place. If you want to really get brave, ask your subconscious to help you remember the reasons why you have anxiety to begin with. When doing this, a scene from your past may materialize. You might see, hear, or feel something in response to your query. If this is the case and you are taken back to an earlier time in your life, see or imagine those events in a different perspective. Tell yourself that you are now free from those events and that they can no longer hurt you. You may want to reimagine them in a positive light. Here's an example of a person who was held up at gunpoint, which can cause a lot of anxiety. If that person relives this experience, they may want to replay it as empowering. They may see themselves being held up and taking the weapon away from the assailant, throwing them to the ground, calling the police, and seeing the individual arrested. This is your playground now, and you can relive scenes from the past the way you want to, even if they didn't happen that way. You may say, "but I'm lying to myself," yes, you are, and I remind you that the subconscious does not know the difference between real and imagined. (Remember what you feel from movies?) Besides, do you realize that you are lying to yourself when you feel anxiety? As previously discussed, anxious feelings are an illusion, so now you are lying to yourself in a good way. Whatever happened is a thing of the past, and you are forever free from it.

If you don't want to dig into your past, it's okay. It's not easy to go back there, especially with trauma. Simply give yourself subconscious suggestions, but start with releasing all experiences as we did above. Below, I list some examples; you are welcome to create your own.

Things like:

- It is easy to release any and all negative emotions I feel in my body.
- I allow any anxious feelings to flow through me without causing any negative effects.

- Everyday I feel more and more sure of myself without the need to connect to any fearful emotions.
- I no longer need anxious feelings to protect me from anything. My inner strength is my protector.
- I always have a deep feeling of safety and security.
- If I feel any anxiety at all, I release it immediately with ease.

When you say them in self-hypnosis, stick to three maximum and repeat them in your mind as many times as you'd like to use the compounding effect. Make sure to say your suggestions with intention, feeling every word, letting it penetrate your very being. After the affirmations, use that opportunity to play out mental scenarios where you release any anxious feelings. Try to conjure them and see if anything comes up in the stomach or chest. The moment you feel something, give that area an opening and let the feelings go. This will give the techniques you are practicing a lot more strength as you work on a subconscious level. You will also come from a position of power when you are in a relaxed, peaceful state because when you are in a deeply relaxed mental state, nothing can bother you. You are grounded, feel confident, and see problems as just things you have to work out. The conscious mind is the one who instigates the endless loop of questions that agitate the mind. The subconscious is a safe space since its job is only to house ideas and protect you from what it perceives is a threat; its job is not to analyze it, only absorb information without judging right or wrong. It may do a low-level analysis of incoming information but nowhere near the level of the conscious mind. Finally, have fun. This is an exciting process where you are literally working directly with that part of you which holds your mental programming. It's exciting to let go of the old, useless programming and replace it with a way of life that will serve you well.

Can I stay in hypnosis forever?

To ease your mind, no way has that ever happened. There is an old belief that you can somehow get "stuck" in the hypnotic state, probably because of what happens from time to time to stage hypnotists. Here's what happens. The hypnotist tells the hypnotized person "when I count to 3, you'll come out of the hypnotized state feeling great. 1...2...3...then nothing happens, and the subject doesn't respond. If you are watching this from an audience member's perspective it could be scary. If a hypnotist doesn't know how to deal with this situation, it could really throw him/her off causing panic. Luckily, Dave Elman covered this scenario in his book and gives an easy way to rouse the person. This scenario happened to me once as I was doing a group demonstration and luckily I knew what to do in order to rouse that person.

In these scenarios here's what happens: There are a small number of people who become so relaxed when they enter hypnosis that they don't want to come out. It feels too good, so when they are asked to come out by the hypnotist, they keep their eyes closed. When this happens on stage in front of an audience, it scares them, causing the belief that you can get stuck in hypnosis forever. If the hypnotist doesn't know what to do about it, they would most likely have someone carry the person off the stage, causing more of an alarm to the spectators. In fact, when a person chooses to hold on to hypnosis, you can move their body, and they will stay in that state for as long as they choose as long as they know they are safe. Keep in mind what I just mentioned. It's a choice, so don't let this scare you because you do the choosing. Actually, the worst that can happen if you don't want to come out of the hypnotic state is that you'll fall asleep and wake up whenever you are ready. Just make sure you don't miss any appointments. I sincerely hope that you are able to use these techniques successfully as they have served me very well.

CHAPTER 20
Meditation

Until this point, we have explored different ways to help calm the mind from everyday agitation. A tranquil mind results in a calm body and less anxiety, so if it is possible for you to do some meditation either regularly or from time to time, it will only aid in calming the nervous system to reduce anxiety. Meditation has often been associated with religious practices, but it doesn't have to be. In this work, we will only focus on the relaxation aspect of meditation as opposed to any religious practices, as meditation can simply be a means of relaxing the mind to calm racing thoughts. While anxiety raises blood pressure, heart rate, adrenaline, and activates the fight-or-flight response, meditation does the exact opposite. It has a calming effect and even plays a role in healing. The more often the mind gets accustomed to maintaining a calm demeanor, the more likely it is to gravitate towards this behavior. I will not spend too much time on this topic since we already covered self-hypnosis, which is basically a meditative state, but I thought it important to cover it since there are some differences.

What is meditation?
In a nutshell, and basically it's the practice of calming the mind by focusing your attention on breath, sounds outside of you like nature sounds, soundscapes, another person's, or your own inner voice. In chapter 12, I wrote something similar to focusing the attention on something outside of you, but it was in the context of becoming present. The difference is that when your aim is to become present, you focus your mind to stop thoughts by using your senses (seeing, hearing, feeling) to empty your mind. Meditation works at stopping negative

thoughts, but positive thoughts are "permitted," so to speak. I say this jokingly, of course; there are no rules. You can still meditate while emptying your thoughts, but typically, the thoughts are on pleasant things while stimulating the imagination. For example, walking through a lush forest while listening to the wind rushing amongst towering oak trees or feeling the sunshine on your face as you listen to the water lap the shoreline on a tranquil beach. These descriptions make use of intense sounds, images, or feelings to help direct your mind toward relaxation by tapping into the senses.

Ways of Meditation

There are many ways to meditate. Before the internet revolution, you needed to read a book or attend a class to learn how to meditate, but not today. Although there are no lack of books or classes, all you need to do is have the intention to meditate, search for a meditation program on the internet, and voila, you are meditating. There are thousands of free or paid meditation recordings or courses you can access at the tips of your fingers. The important thing is to find something that resonates with you, as not all programs are for everyone. You have to be able to connect with the ideas when something is written, or a voice that you like if listening to a program. If you choose to do this, explore and experiment.

Guided and Self-Guided Meditation

In the wonderful world of meditation, you can choose either guided or self-guided meditation. When being guided, you simply turn on and listen to the operator's voice, whether through recording or live following their instructions. It is easier to start this way since you don't have to do any thinking (the very thing you want to steer away from). I have spoken to many people throughout the years about meditation, and many of them prefer guided because their minds either leap from one idea to another or begin to think about their problems. This is not uncommon as our minds are constantly focused on the things we have to solve in life. It's what gives us a reason to live and exist. I have produced many guided meditation recordings for specific things like falling asleep, improving health, releasing stress, etc. You can find these programs on YouTube if you search for Israel Maya Hypnosis.

Self-Guided meditation is exactly what it sounds like. You guide yourself into a meditative state by the use of your own intentions, thoughts, and inner voice. This requires experience and skill to know how to guide yourself without getting entangled in your own thoughts. It also requires you to be impartial to interruptions from surrounding sounds. With guided meditation, you must have a plan, a purpose, and a means as to how you will guide yourself. As previously mentioned, it takes more skill, so it may not be for beginners. The benefit of being able to guide yourself is that you can go at your own pace as opposed to being forced to move at the pace of the person guiding you. You can also choose what to focus on, whether visiting a place you create in your mind, focusing on better health, opening creativity, or whatever possibilities you can imagine. It's like going on vacation. You either go with a tour guide or you explore on your own. Each has benefits and drawbacks.

Meditation for Anxiety
Meditation can also be used to help lessen anxiety. Having the concept of compounding in mind (or a repetition of an action or suggestion to create a change in the subconscious), the more often you meditate when you are not in an anxious state, the more accustomed your body and mind become to being calm. We are creatures of habit, so if you repeatedly do something that makes you calm, you are most likely going to have calmer demeanor. I know that by now if I were to ask you why this happens, you would be able to tell me that it is because repetition pushes actions and reactions into the subconscious mind in order for those reactions to become automatic in the

future. (You're so smart.) It doesn't matter whether the reactions we have are positive or negative.

The following is a personal example of a negative subconscious reaction I used to have based on something that happened to me in my younger years. I once attended a synagogue where, when the religious leader would give his weekly sermon, he spoke badly about the president of the institution in front of him. When the president gave his announcements, he also spoke badly about the religious leader in front of him. This caused a tremendous amount of discomfort as what was being said was delivered candidly and with a smile but with a heavy dosage of sarcasm. Some community members found it comical, but I felt very uncomfortable every time each one of them would speak. After some time, my body began to react by sweating because I believe that a house of worship is not the place to air out frustrations for one another especially in public. I became so uncomfortable with their unkind remarks for each other that when either one would get up to speak, I immediately began to sweat before they would say anything. This was my subconscious reacting automatically. I had gotten so used to reacting this way that it became an auto-response. This is something similar to Pavlov's dog. We have these reactions all the time and are not aware of them, again because they are subconscious. The smell of food is one of them. When we smell food, it triggers a hunger response, etcetera. Like these, there are many, but since our focus is to create pleasant responses, meditation is one positive way to create a more favorable way of responding to life in general.

What happens if you fall asleep during meditation?

I hope that by now you have come to understand that absolutely nothing bad can happen to you while in hypnosis, self-hypnosis, or meditation. I group them together here because they are all basically the same brainwave state. The difference is how you are guided, or self-guided in this state, that will determine your outcome of the mental relaxation exercise. If it wasn't apparent in previous pages, I want to put your mind completely at ease and assure you that you cannot stay "stuck" in any of these states. The "worse" that can happen when doing any type of deep mental relaxation is that you will fall asleep and wake up whenever your brain tells you that it's time to. That's it! If you were doing some kind of guided imagery while meditating, you may possibly dream about whatever you were imagining last.

As mentioned in chapter 8 of this book, the hypnotic or meditative state is just a state of relaxation every human being passes through when they are falling asleep or waking up. It is a completely natural state. We don't usually experience it for longer periods of time more often because unless trained or experimenting, it is not a typical state to hold onto. It is only used as a doorway to sleep or waking up. It's like using your legs. You can use them to walk most of your life, and they will get you from point A to B just fine. You can also use them to run giving them a different function. The deeper states of consciousness are always there for you waiting to be discovered. You just have to tap into them and they are there.

CHAPTER 21
Alternative Forms of Relaxation

∽

Massage

Massage is an excellent way to help your body and mind relax. It is obvious, but not everyone thinks of it. Plus, if you don't have the financial means, it gets expensive. I remember when I was working on my anxiety issues that a massage session would cost $60-$80, but this was some decades back. A good massage therapist can cost you $100-$150 per session (perhaps less in a massage parlor), and if you are going through major anxiety, you'll need 2-3 sessions per week. Again, if you don't have the financial means, you are looking at $200-$450 a week plus the investment of time, but if money is not an issue, you are okay. The benefits are obvious in how a good massage helps to reduce anxiety. It aids in relaxation by releasing muscle tension and endorphins. You also sleep better with a more relaxed body, which has a ripple effect for the next day, so I suggest a massage at night if possible. Additionally, the human touch of a caring massage therapist brings healing on its own as they transfer their good intentions to you and your body. The human touch cannot be overlooked, not in a sexual or sensual way, but in reference to healing. We all need to be touched (unless we have some kind of trauma about it), and a good massage fulfills that need.

When I was going through anxiety some decades ago, I set up several sessions of massage, and they did help in reducing the tension that my body accumulated from anxiety. It's obvious that as you tense your body from over-stressing and overthinking, your muscles tighten, and they return to their relaxed state by themselves, especially when it happens often. It's almost as if you have to force them back to relaxation or remind them "hey relax." Surely you are aware that it comes to a point where you don't even notice how tense your body gets, so a good massage helps to loosen this tightness. I actually dated a massage therapist for a while, which may make you think that I'd get a lot of free massages...jackpot! It's quite the opposite, though. The running joke of one dating a massage therapist is that you get more massages as a client than from a partner. In all fairness though, massage therapy is tiresome on the operator, and they don't want to come home to start working again; they just want to relax, so I understand why they wouldn't want to give a partner a massage.

If finances are an issue and you are not able to hire a massage therapist or go to a massage parlor, no need to worry. There are very good, much less expensive options that you could look into. The most expensive is a massage chair. We've evolved from tables that have rollers on them which go back and forth on your back, to pads which vibrate and, at the time of this writing, a massage chair that is capable of practically delivering a full-body massage.

Massage Chairs
A massage chair can cost $2000-$5000. Wait! Before you think, "Wow, that's expensive." Yes, it is, but there are people that bought massage chairs who now want to get rid of them because they no longer use them. You can buy a used one on social media marketplaces (proceed with caution), and it will be considerably less than a new one. If you have some money saved up and prefer a new chair, then jump on the internet or Amazon, and you can get one delivered straight to your home. I personally don't have one (yet), but whenever I go on a trip, I spring the $5 it costs to get 15 minutes on the massage chairs

in the airport. The ones at the airport aren't great but good enough to loosen some muscles. I have been on chairs that will blow you away with all the muscle groups they massage. It's fascinating!

Guns, Pads, Massagers

A much cheaper option for massage if you don't want to put a large chair in your home is a massage gun, pad, or massagers that work on the neck and back, or feet. These are inexpensive options that take up much less space, and range from $40 to $200. I love massage guns because they help you target areas of your body for longer periods of time without relying on rollers that will only pass through. The massage guns they have today last a long time on a single charge and have very high settings. I never go above 3 of 9 when massaging different areas of my body. The fancier ones deliver heat or even cold. I don't use the gun for anxiety reduction, rather to release any muscle tension from the neck and shoulders as those are common areas to tighten. I often massage just the bottom of my feet and that alone helps me sleep very deeply. Besides the release of muscle tension, the use of massage guns can help release emotional tension trapped in the body. This phenomenon occurs with regular massage therapy when the operator presses or massages a certain spot in the body and the one receiving either begins to laugh or cry. The theory is that emotions get trapped in muscles and when stimulated the emotion is released, and this happens with mechanical massage and/ or the massage gun. Whichever route you choose, either one gives you a good option to act as another tool to combat anxiety.

Acupuncture

I can't remember a time when I got acupuncture and didn't fall asleep. I don't know what it is exactly, but for me, perhaps the points that are stimulated with the needles help me to let go in a way that is so deep I end up falling asleep every time. You know how acupuncture works, right? It's done with long, thin needles inserted into certain parts of your body to stimulate targeted energy points. There are a standard of over three hundred points, with some practitioners recognizing over two thousand points all over the body. I've had needles simultaneously placed in my face, ear, feet, top of my head, arms, and legs. Does it hurt? I guess it depends on how you define hurt. Some needles pinch a little bit, but you hardly feel most of them, so they are not painful. I would say there is a little discomfort for the most part, but for me the discomfort doesn't last long. The understanding behind acupuncture is deep and beyond the scope of this work, but I think it's definitely worth trying a few sessions to see how much it can lessen your anxiety. Not everyone responds the same to every treatment, so what works for me may not work for you in the same way, but again it's worth a try. The important thing to note here is that acupuncture is another alternative form of treatment for many ailments and can definitely be helpful to lessen anxiety. Are there any side effects with acupuncture? Yes, there can be, like possible bleeding at the site of a needle, bruising, or possibly a little soreness. Most likely, though, you won't have any of these with a competent practitioner, unless your skin is super sensitive. Keep in mind that the needles are as thin as a hair (or slightly thinner), so there isn't much to feel with something this thin. Finances are also a factor, as with massage, since a treatment may cost $80-$120, but I believe that the frequency of treatment may be less with one to two sessions per week. It's difficult to say obviously with each practitioner having their own method and opinion as to how to treat their patients, but as I mentioned before it's definitely worth giving it a try to see if this is a good fit for you. Acupuncturists are usually versed in some kind of Chinese medicine, herbology, or natural remedy. If you visit a practitioner, don't be surprised if they recommend some kind of remedy or tea to treat your anxiety.

We'll talk about safe, easy-to-obtain herbal remedies for anxiety a bit further in this chapter.

Working Out or Exercise

It seems that with any fear-based emotion we tend to stop what we are doing as fear makes us freeze or stop in our tracks. That being the case (not for everyone), doing the opposite like working out or exercising may help to ease the nervous tension. If you belong to a gym or can start going, it can be very beneficial for you to put any nervous energy to good use while you not only burn off the extra nervous energy but also gain strength and muscle while you are at it. A good workout or exercise routine can help to lessen anxiety because it tires you out and allows your body and muscles to relax once you are finished. If done during the daytime, it can help to boost your energy levels; if done at nighttime, it can help you relax because you are already tired from the day. Plus, having anxiety is exhausting as it causes your nervous system to rev up into a frenzy, so working off that extra energy might just be what you need.

Herbal Remedies

Herbs are something that is very near and dear to my heart since I use them all the time for healing. When I was in my twenties (a long time ago), I took an antibiotic for a sticky fever that did me a world of damage. It seemed like the more medication I took, the worse I got, so some people I met who later became good friends told me about the power of herbs. I was ignorant on the topic and didn't know such a world existed until I began to investigate more. Imagine that, the only remedies I knew were drug-based, but because my body was intolerant to harsh medication, I had no choice but to learn an alternative means to heal my body. In reality, the alternative means is the synthetic drugs since herbs came first. Just like pharmaceutical drugs, herbs have an effect which targets different parts of the body. The effect is obviously not as quick as with drugs, but it can be as potent and as healing depending upon what is being targeted and which medication is being taken. As I mentioned before, I respect the time and place for synthetic medication, but the overuse and abuse of meds can be quite destructive to the human body, as many people unfortunately find out. There are drugs to take care of the side effects of drugs, so what does that tell you? Herbs are gentler on the body and easier to tolerate. Are there herbs that can have harsh effects on the body? Yes, there are, but it's less likely, especially if you proceed with caution and have a little knowledge of what you are doing or taking. The point here is that herbs are much safer, and your body is a lot more forgiving if you take an herbal remedy that doesn't agree with you.

Before I mention the names of any herbs, I want to caution you. Please ensure you conduct thorough research and consult your healthcare provider, doctor, or practitioner to make sure that these substances are suitable for you. Although herbs are generally considered milder and safer than drugs, they are potent and may or may not have interactions with other medications you are taking, so please take the extra precaution and do your due diligence.

That being said, I found that when I was going through anxiety, there were certain herbs I took that would either help lessen the intensity of the anxiety or eliminate it altogether for a period of time. One of those herbs is valerian root. This was always my go-to herb whenever I had the onset of any anxiety. It is known for centuries to help calm the nervous system and is used for sleep by many. The positive side effect is that once absorbed in the body, it has a calming effect. When I first started taking valerian, I'd feel calm and a bit of a high from it. I was still able to focus just fine, but it made me feel happy as if the troubles of my world were all going to work themselves out just fine (as they usually do). Some people may feel sleepy after taking it as it acts like a mild sedative, but if you are revved up from anxiety, it just might balance you out. If you feel too sleepy from taking it, then it might be a good idea to only take it at night when you are already home or before you go to bed. It's impossible to know what effects you'll have from it until you take it, so once you've determined that it's safe for you to take and have consulted a healthcare practitioner, buy a bottle from a reputable company of your local health food store and follow directions on the bottle. Just make sure to stop taking it if you experience any adverse effects from this or any other herb.

You can take this herb in three different ways: a capsule, tincture, or tea form. Encapsulated (in a double O cap) is the more common form of taking the herb, but if you prefer not to take a capsule, you can take it in tincture form. The tincture is a concentrated liquid sold in a few ounces that is either mixed with alcohol (to improve absorption) or vegetable glycerin. The tincture is convenient as a handful of drops (20-30) can have the effect you are looking for, and as capsules it's easy to take with you wherever you go. If you like tea, steeping the herb or tea bag gives you the essence and effect with the added benefit of sipping it slowly along with something sweet like cookies or a piece of cake. The downside of tea is that you don't get a definitive dosage; and it's not as concentrated as the other forms. Also, you should know valerian doesn't have the most pleasant smell, but the interesting thing about this herb (for me anyway) is that the smell of it never matches the taste. For me the tea or tincture has more of a neutral taste along with the odd smell.

Another go-to herb which I really liked and used quite often is skullcap. This herb is milder than valerian but just as effective. It is apparently a part of the mint family and can be taken in the same way as you take valerian root (capsule, tincture, tea), but it doesn't have the same sleepy effect that valerian does. Keep in mind that everyone responds in their own way, so while for some it doesn't make sleepy, for others, it might. For those which valerian makes too sleepy, skullcap can be used in the daytime, while valerian at night. In combination, these herbs can really take the anxiety edge off as they are both used to treat it by many practitioners. Other herbs or substances that are milder to help promote calm are chamomile, linden (Tilo), and L-theanine, which is an amino acid. You may also find these mixed together in herbal capsule remedies.

Which one is better? They are all good. I mentioned valerian and skullcap first because those were the ones I learned about and used, but I have used chamomile tea, linden tea, and L-theanine amino acid in a chewable, and capsule form. The important thing here is to find what works best for you if this is one of the routes you'd like to explore. These herbal remedies or substances are a mixture of vitamins and minerals which come together to create the plant you are ingesting. From a physical standpoint, your body is never deficient in aspirin or anti-anxiety drugs; it is more likely deficient in a vitamin, mineral, or amino acid which, when taken, helps to balance you out or bring more stability to your body and nervous system. There are times where prescription medication creates an imbalance in your body, so using synthetic substances should be approached with caution and knowledge. I'm not giving you medical advice, and I'm not badmouthing the pharmaceutical industry; as previously stated, they all have their time and place. I'm simply calling a different perspective to your attention. Generally speaking, these herbal remedies are safe, and if you took something that doesn't agree with you or, let's say, you "overdosed" or took too much valerian, the most that would probably happen is that you get too sleepy, have a stomach ache, or maybe a little diarrhea. All of these suggestions are just more tools in your toolbox. I want you to feel like you don't have to settle and are limited to only one solution. Written above, you have many solutions and many different angles that you can approach the problem. For me, each one was another gift. I hope it will be like this for you as well.

CHAPTER 22

Maybe it's your liver.

∽

Here's an important topic that is definitely overlooked...your liver. All of the organs in the body are important, so I'm not going to say that it's the most important. It is, however, overlooked when it comes to anxiety because no one would ever look there if they were experiencing it. The liver cleanses the blood, and almost everything that we ingest passes through it, especially when it has to be filtered, so why would anyone look at a filter when focusing on a mental condition, right? We all believe anxiety to be a condition of the mind, but we both know that's not always the case. Body and mind work together. If one is bothered, the other will be too. There's only one doctor who ever agreed with me, saying an intoxicated liver can cause anxiety, so when I heard it from him, my eyes lit up because it happened to me.

Besides the lifelong anxiety I experienced, what I felt exacerbated it was an antibiotic I was taking at one point for a sticky fever I had in my 20s. I spoke about it briefly in the last chapter. That's when I got into herbology. Nonetheless, when things got worse and the anxiety ramped up, I really felt within me that the antibiotic was a making things worse. I went to see a medical doctor, and he thought I was totally wrong, (and probably crazy) but I still went with my gut instinct. The problem I was having lasted for quite some time, but eventually I recovered. A bit over a decade later, I was separated from my ex-wife, stayed at a friend's home, and started to drink some alcohol he had in his cabinet, thinking it would help numb some of what I was going through. What ended up happening was that my liver went into major crisis mode. The drinking was minimal, never enough to get drunk, but whatever I did pushed my poor liver over the edge. My right side would swell at least once per day, I'd get fever-like symptoms, and my heart would pound like crazy. It was horrible, and with all of this came anxiety....lots of it, like copious amounts. I felt validated in what I believed. A liver that's under attack from either alcohol or medicine that it doesn't like can cause anxiety. This happened to me a third time when on a few Friday nights I drank 1 ounce of very mild 5% alcohol wine for about 6 weeks. Mind you, it was only 1 time per week, and just one ounce. I liked the taste, and my family was drinking as well. They were all fine, but it didn't work out so well for me. At the end of 6 weeks, I'd wake up at around 3-4 in the morning with my heart pounding and my blood pressure through the roof. It was an extremely uncomfortable experience, but it was comforting to know that the problem I was going through was indeed coming from my liver. It felt attacked again and was acting out like a teenager screaming for attention, saying "daaaad uh, what are you doing uh?" (You know, how they talk?) I stopped the alcohol immediately and knew that my last sip of wine would literally be my last forever. No more guessing or theorizing. I had all the confirmation I needed and knew that if I ever drank alcohol again or had to take any medication, I was in for more episodes. Interestingly enough, what helped to bring my blood pressure down was acupuncture. Yeah, who would have thought, right? Nonetheless, with the help of the acupuncturist and the techniques I teach here, my symptoms faded until they became an old memory that remained untouched unless I told this story.

Some people still dismissed my theory, but I didn't care. I knew I was right. I once visited a doctor for a checkup, and he said, "You're allergic to alcohol." "Yes!" I said. I had the right words to tell everyone who offered me a drink. I'm allergic. That's perfect. You don't know how annoying it is to be at a party or get together, and someone offers you a drink. They offer. You say no. They offer again. You still say no. Then they look at you funny, "You sure?" "Yes, no, thank you." It's a whole to-do. Now I just say, "I'm allergic," and they just look at me and say.... "Ohh." In any case, now you know and have very important information that you may not have been offered either by your doctor or health care provider. An unhappy liver can cause some serious anxiety.

What can you do if you are experiencing this? If it's alcohol, stop drinking any and all alcoholic beverages for some time. I mean months. If your liver is under attack, it will need time to recover. If you are taking medication and this is happening, then stop if you can, but obviously with the guidance of your doctor. Some people like to take pills with the first sign of well....anything. Headache-pill, a little cough-pill, a cold-pill. I suggest you find an alternative means, especially if your liver is sensitive. Most people are okay with meds, those who aren't will have to be much more careful. I know, this is how I live, not that I regret it. In fact, I appreciate taking natural remedies to resolve physical issues. I feel my body is happier and healthier because of it. Some conditions will need meds, but those that don't can be resolved through natural means.

I once passed a kidney stone. It was the most powerful pain I've ever experienced. I didn't know what was happening at the time, but when I went to the emergency room, I knew they would have to give me something at least for the pain. They gave me morphine. The doctor suggested 4 mg; I said, "Give me 2, and we'll see what happens." I told them I have a very sensitive liver, so I have to be very cautious as to what goes into my body. They agreed and were very compassionate. The 2mg did the trick. It blocked the pain almost instantly, and when it came back a few hours later, I asked for 2 more milligrams. Again, it worked like magic, and after a few hours, the stone passed. I also received a medicine that dilated my ureters and something as an anti-nausea. All were tolerated well. I think for me it's long-term medication use that does the damage. Short-term can be tolerated, but long-term can have some serious side effects. If you are experiencing anxiety after heavy drinking or medication use, please consider this information. It could be life-changing.

CHAPTER 23

Be Kind to Yourself

∾

We have covered so many topics in this book, and we are both working hard to break preconceived notions, habits, and beliefs. By now, if you've followed my understanding and philosophy, you'll know that anxiety is just an illusion, which is as real as a dream. You know when you wake up with a pounding heart or tears in your eyes from a scary or sad dream? It seems very real, but it is just an illusion and a figment of your imagination. There are no characters in your dreams except you. You are you, and the other good and bad characters. Nonetheless, we react to the dream, believing that it is really happening to us until we wake up and say, "Whew, thank goodness it was just a dream." You feel it and go through difficulties, but ultimately realize it's not real. The same applies to anxiety. You feel it deeply within you and react to thoughts or situations, but when you calm down, you come to the realization that everything is okay.

What I have presented to you in the last 20 chapters is how to deal with it and live your life without the anxious state. For some who read the ideas at the beginning of the book, especially in chapter 4, the ideas may cause struggle or challenge in them. "How can you say that what I'm feeling is a ghost, phantasm, or an illusion?" one may say. It can even bring anger, but when seen from a logical standpoint, it is simply a way to look at something that doesn't exist. You should ask questions like "What is making me so anxious?" and "Does it make sense to be so afraid?" "What can I do to make myself feel better from what I feel?" Most of the time, we don't ask ourselves these questions and are just swept away by a wild emotion that has the power to make us forget logic. When you begin to see the light, however your eyes open, your perspective changes, and you see your world in a different way. At the beginning, you may teeter back and forth, walking on unsteady ground. You may have good days and days that are not so good, as old patterns and subconscious messages creep back into your conscious mind. You might just have a great morning, waking up with bold ideas that allow you to feel amazing without the gripping hold of anxiety, and then slip back to it in the afternoon. When you experience the success you want and then fall back, be gentle with yourself. Don't get upset and don't beat yourself up. You are walking a new path, and that on its own means that you have to change your identity. Our subconscious mind holds a persona that we carefully construct year after year from the moment of birth. The ideas that we hold so near and dear to our hearts may not always be the ones that are beneficial to a healthy lifestyle or psyche. When we realize that we have to let some of these ideas go, it becomes scary. It means we have to change, and change for many people is not easy even if what they are changing from is hurting them.

Keep in mind that you are already brave for taking the necessary steps to confront your anxiety, examine it, work with it, even accept it, uproot it, and release it. That takes guts. Take that in. Internalize what I just said and really think about it for a moment. Most people will do anything they can to bury the feelings or suppress them, but not you. You have taken the approach of the warrior. Your armor is the knowledge you acquire, and the more knowledge you have about this condition, the stronger your armor gets and the more tools you obtain. You gain armament, and techniques to use in order to combat anxiety until it releases its hold. If lack of knowledge was an impediment before, it's not anymore.

Now you have an arsenal of useful tools you can use to help you live a life of freedom: understanding, mental techniques, the aid of professionals, and herbs. This is how I did it. I used every possible tool at my disposal and didn't stop until I reached my goal. Pause for a moment and breathe in freedom. It's inside of you, and all around you. There is no reason you can't own it; it's already yours! Remember our comparison of peace and sounds in chapter 6? Where is peace? It's right where you are. The disturbance of your inner peace is your thoughts, but just because you don't feel peaceful doesn't mean that peace isn't with you. It is always with you. You are still getting used to a new way of thinking and lifestyle, so again be gentle with yourself, and if you slip backwards, don't worry. Don't speak harshly to yourself, get frustrated, or think you're doing something wrong. Once you understand this process and begin to live it, slipping back only means that your mind is fighting the change, which is normal. The more you release this resistance, the closer you are to the peace you are ready to enjoy.

Celebrate Every Win

As mentioned in this chapter, once you begin your healing process you'll begin to notice that there will be a few hours of the day, an entire day or even days in which you'll feel great and no anxiety is present. All of a sudden it doesn't have the same effect on you as it did before. As you are on your way to these moments of freedom, celebrate them. Be cognizant and aware when you are feeling well and acknowledge those moments. If its five minutes then celebrate those five minutes because every win in your book should count as a big win. Doing this, you attach positive feelings to winning, your brain begins to associate what you consider good and you create more of those wins. Often times we tend to look at what's wrong with the world as opposed to what is right. If you've experienced this behavior then it's time for a change. Look at what is right because I can guarantee you that when you have anxiety you are not looking for the most positive things in your life. Besides sucking the life out of you, anxiety forces you to look at what is wrong in your life otherwise you'd be happy. It's time to celebrate those great moments because haven't you suffered enough?

CHAPTER 24

It's Your Choice

∞

I'm sure you've met people who have told you about a problem they have or are having, and you try to give them advice, but their response is "What can I do? This is just the way I am." I've come across many people like this, and when I meet people with this attitude, I stay clear from giving them advice because with their response, I accept that they are exercising their freedom of choice. We all have it, and with that, you have the right to choose how you live your life, how you think, and how you respond to life's difficulties. Anxiety is a difficult condition to live with, no doubt, but with all of the tools, knowledge, and technology available to us, it shouldn't be. Each individual has to ultimately make the decision to either continue living with this condition or to let it go. Is it easy to let go? Of course not; it takes a lot of work to change the way we feel and think about a condition that may've started decades, or years ago. Nonetheless, the benefits of such hard work certainly outweighs the amount of time and effort necessary to get there. In the end, it is ultimately your choice to hold on to or let go of anxiety.

Some people may read this book and say, "This is too much for me; I can't do this." My response would be the same to all: "Is living with anxiety better?" Part of my job as a hypnotherapist was to contradict my patients if they didn't want to heal or let go of what was giving them trouble. I wanted them to heal; that's why they came to me, and my wishes are that you heal as well. I understand that you want to heal from anxiety, or at least some part of you wants to. Otherwise, you would neither have picked up this book nor have gotten this far. In any case, I want you to know that I respect your decision. I prefer that you adopt this new philosophy, go through the exercises, explore alternative means, and get the help you need, but again, I will also respect your decision wherever you want to proceed from here as you have that right to choose. Some people feel that it's not the right time to heal, and I honor that decision as well. I clearly remember a woman who came to do hypnosis with me (not anxiety-related) and did a tremendous amount of healing in our first session. I asked her to come back for a second session because she was still holding on to anger and needed to work through it. She agreed that she needed to let it go, but she didn't come back. I was puzzled as to why she cancelled her session, scheduled for the upcoming week. It turns out, she called me one year later and said she wanted to schedule another appointment. When I asked her why she waited so long, she said that she felt she was not ready to let go of the anger that was eating her up inside. The anger was not only part of her identity, but something she felt gave her strength. She expressed that without it she would become weak. When she returned to my office, she was ready to change that angry person she had been for so long. Either way, I told her she was brave for choosing to be the angry self and brave for now choosing to let go.

The human experience is a difficult one because we wrestle with so many emotions. Everything could be fine one moment, and all of a sudden, our emotions change. Life could be fine, and from one moment to the next, things can happen to make major changes either for the better or worse. If we don't have the skill and ability to self-regulate, we become overloaded with emotions that shut down our thinking and push away logic. We then act recklessly and at times go on a path of self-destruction. This entire book has been about empowerment, to help you get off the self-destructive path so that you can have more balance in your life. It aims at empowering you to let you know that you are literally the only one who can walk yourself out of the labyrinthine maze you are in. At first, it feels impossible, confusing and tiresome. The more you work at it, though the easier it becomes to find your way to the end of that maze. I hope you choose the road I've mapped out for you because in the end, the hardest path really becomes the easiest.

Will I be able to get rid of all anxiety forever?
We all have that tendency to get anxious when we face a new challenge. It could be the start of a new job, getting up on stage, asking our loved one's hand in marriage, sitting at the doctor's office while waiting for results, or going to the bank to get a loan. All of these have the same common denominator: the unknown. Whenever we are faced with the unknown, we have the tendency to get anxious because it's nerve-wracking to wait for an answer or outcome. I'm sure you can relate to the following: "and the winner is....." Even if you are not the contestant, there is a possibility for you to get even a little anxious as you watch a competition waiting for the response. You want the lady in the blue dress to win, so you get anxious for her. It's not an anxiety that's crippling, and it won't follow you around, but it's still a slight anxiety.

I'm pretty sure most will agree that anxiety is hardwired into our system to keep us on our toes and prepare us for what's coming (whatever that may be). It's part of the internal and innate fight or flight system that helps us survive when we get into some kind of trouble, or when trouble finds us. If it didn't exist, we may not survive certain encounters, for example, an active shooter. At the onset of an active shooter situation, we deny what is happening, but when we realize that this is real, the anxiety causes adrenaline to dump into your system for a fight or flight response. You are either going to run to survive or fight for your life. This anxiety is necessary.

To answer the original question of this section, no. You can't get rid of all anxiety forever as it wouldn't be safe. We can call the anxiety described above as healthy anxiety. It is in place to help us survive, and eradicating it would be unwise. The anxiety we want to get rid of is the senseless one that keeps us constantly worrying about things that will probably never happen or ones you have control over. For example: a plane crashing into our house, a break-in, getting mugged on the street, worry about getting emotionally hurt with every friend you have— you get the idea. These things are possible, like getting mugged, especially if you walk around in an area where it is prone to happen. Break-ins are very common no matter what neighborhood you live in, so how do you avoid having anxiety about things that can actually happen? Logically, you take precautions. Don't walk in dangerous areas by yourself, especially at night. Secure your home, making sure it's always locked. Have situational awareness when you go out in general. Don't open yourself up to the point of vulnerability to your friends or acquaintances so you don't get hurt. You don't have to be anxious, you just have to be aware, and if anxiety is present, then use the tools you have learned to let it go.

There is a big difference between necessary and unnecessary anxiety. One will help you survive, and one doesn't let you live. Then there is also anxiety just for anxiety's sake without any reason. This one is the illusion, and plainly unnecessary in all respects. It most likely has a root cause in the past that has to be examined either consciously or unconsciously and let go. You may find what's lurking in your subconscious in a hypnosis session, a self-hypnosis, meditation, or just by reminiscing about the past. It is the one that when released will liberate you. To sum up, anxiety is actually a good thing in place for our survival but it's not healthy to have at all times, any one of our emotions are the same. Too much of any emotion is not healthy and impractical. Can you imagine being happy at a funeral, or sad at a birthday party? Imagine crying at a comedy show or laughing when someone tells you how awful a day they are having. See what I mean? We have emotions that have limitations in time because we exist in time. There's a time for everything and boundaries have to be set so that we can have balance in this world. To re-quote from The Matrix Revolutions, "Everything that has a beginning has an end." Whether intended like this or not there is a great lesson to be learned from just this line. If it starts, it's going to stop, so to give you comfort for any anxiety you are having, one day it will be over. It may take time, it may be difficult, you may have to work hard at it but it will be over because like anything in this world it is finite.

If you want freedom give freedom.
Here we circle back around to letting things go. It is the most fundamental action that will give you freedom. I want you to really think about this and keep it in mind because this helped me tremendously as well. When something is under pressure leaving when you give it an opening, it is looking for an escape. Don't worry, I'll explain. Think of a pressure cooker or flowing water. Either one is a good analogy. With any one of these, they are looking for an escape, movement, a way out, and if it doesn't find it, it gets stuck. These are your feelings. They are looking for a way out of your body. How do I know? When you give it an opening, they leave, don't they? This is how you can tell that they are under pressure. If you want to be free from anxiety or any negative feeling, you must first give those feelings their freedom. Once you allow them to leave, you will feel free as well. This was a very powerful lesson for me and one that helped propel the release of less desirous feelings. Simply put: if you want freedom, give freedom, and you'll have it.

CHAPTER 25

Get More of What You Want

∽

It was several months after having broken up with an ex-girlfriend, and I was feeling great. (I'll leave you to interpret.) I moved into an apartment where I lived on my own, got myself all new furniture, and set up the place just the way I wanted. I changed the outlets, the chandelier, and the kitchen. For me, the place looked and felt perfect. What was next? It was time for me to appreciate everything I had, so I made a list of 10 things that I really appreciated in my life and read that list in the morning and at night. I read them with feeling and intention, internalizing every word because I truly felt a deep gratitude for everything that Gd had given me. Not too long after, I began to notice that the more I appreciated what I had, the more of it I received. I came to the conclusion that if you have great things in your life (and we all have many) and you don't appreciate them, we can lose them. For me, the reason is spiritual. I believe (and you don't have to agree if you don't want) that to some extent, we bring into our life experience those things that we focus on. If we focus on positive things, they intensify, and if we focus on negative things, the same happens. Appreciating the good we have in our lives is a very potent way to place our attention to what is important. How does this relate to anxiety? The same way we spoke about celebrating in chapter 21. If you have even a little moment in time where you don't have anxiety, celebrate it! In this case, give your fondest and deepest appreciation to the fact that you are feeling well. The appreciation you give shows how you are savoring the release from suffering and anchoring the euphoric feeling of tasting freedom to letting go.

To look at this from a more logical perspective: focusing your attention on anything causes it to "expand" because you are fixating your thoughts on something specific, and your brain pays attention to it. It's like getting a specific new car. You never noticed how many of them there were of those on the road, but now that you have one and your mind is fixated on that model (because you are excited about it), you see more of them. By appreciating the lack of anxiety, you direct your attention to a positive feeling, which in turn anchors itself to a feeling of freedom. The freedom is what you feel from not having anxiety. Training your brain in this fashion will cause you to have less anxiety over time. Again, this is one more technique or tool that you are using in conjunction with the other things you've learned.

Anxiety Changes
When something occurs which can cause anxiety and it is not resolved, the anxiety can change into something else and extend itself to different areas of your life. For example, if one were to get trapped in an elevator because it got stuck, it can be a scary experience. Some may dismiss it after the elevator starts working again and all is well. However, some may keep that fear inside and may replay it in their heads, causing anxiety in other similar areas. If the fear is not resolved, it has the potential to turn into an anxiety that expands to a fear of being in a small room, for example, a closet, or turn into a fear of being on a plane.

This actually happened to a client of mine, we'll call her Debra. Debra made an appointment with me for a fear of flying she wanted resolved. In the intake interview she told me that she was always fine with the idea of flying all the way up to when the plane doors closed. Once she knew the doors had closed, she began to get anxious. I found this to be interesting and simply jotted it down as I usually do. While in the hypnotic state, she regressed to an earlier childhood memory, and described remembering and seeing (in her mind's eye) herself as a child in the kitchen of her house in Cuba many years ago. The oven she had still used hot coals, and Debra's mother would put her in the kitchen when she misbehaved, closed the wooden windows, and make it super dark. Mom would leave her by herself in the kitchen as punishment and told her that the glowing embers of the hot coals were the eyes of demons watching her, waiting to get her because she misbehaved. This was not only a horrible experience, but really stupid of her mother. Unfortunately, this is the way people used to think. They thought that scaring their children was a good way to discipline them. Little Debra was terrorized and internalized those experiences. When she grew up, the closing of the plane doors symbolized the closing of the kitchen windows in her mind, which stirred her subconscious fears. Later in life, she dismissed the kitchen incident as anything that may've caused psychological harm, but she was petrified when those plane doors closed. Her subconscious was trying to protect her from the demons her mother told her about, so it created anxiety as a form of protection. The fear of anything happening to her was an illusion in which she didn't know where it was coming from. The truth is there was no misbehaving, there were no demons, and she was no longer in the kitchen of her old Cuban house. She was enclosed in the fuselage of a plane, but for whatever reason, her subconscious associated being on the plane to her old kitchen. Nonetheless, when she understood all of this, she was able to heal from the kitchen incident while in hypnosis, and flying became a breeze later (no pun intended). We used hypnotic techniques to accept what happened in the past as ignorance from her mother's part, and something that was isolated, which could no longer harm her. Once she released it, she healed and was able to fly on a plane without any fears. It only took 2 sessions to heal years of fears because we used logic and the natural-born ability all humans have to release.

Anxiety is not the enemy.

With all the bad press that anxiety receives, (and we've given it) it's important to note that anxiety is not something you have to fight against and is not your enemy. In this case, there is no enemy. It may seem as if you are fighting your feelings or fighting against something that is destructive, but the truth is you are only fighting yourself. Persistent anxiety is an illusion created by our mind's imagination. Doesn't it make sense that if we believe anxiety to be our enemy, we are only fighting ourselves? You don't want to fight yourself as that puts you in a negative light to well…you. This is similar to the dream analogy. In a dream, you are you, and the rest of the characters in that dream are from your subconscious projections. When you dream about your friend, there is no friend, mother, father, or family member. Even people who you don't recognize in your dreams are simply a projection of your subconscious mind. Nobody else is in your dream but you, so the anxiety you feel is something to accept as something that your subconscious wants to protect you from and release it. Anxiety (for the most part) is not coming from the outside; it's coming from the inside, and only you can control it or, in the best-case scenario, let it go. It may have a root cause that comes from outside of you or the past, for example, if an outside source or event scared you. During or after the event, you internalize it and make it yours. It then gets repeated in your mind, played over and over as a projection of something that you worry may happen in the future. As you have already experienced, the majority of the time those things don't come to pass, and you are safe, yet the fear remains. When you come to this realization, accept it, let it flow through you, and let it go. This will ultimately get you better results than fighting or suppressing it, but you already knew that, didn't you? If you've already tried fighting against it, it's time to try something new: accept it, let it flow through you, and release it. This is what we've been saying throughout this whole work, and the techniques I've taught in the pages above go hand in hand with this approach.

Conclusion

∽

Well, my friend, we've reached the end of this work, but by no means the end of our journey, as it's only the beginning. We've learned how anxiety is something that, even though it feels very real, is just a fear or a projection of the future and, in the most likelihood, will never happen. While these thoughts cause you to react physically and emotionally, you're eventually okay once a little time goes by. Even though you feel like you're going to die with a panic attack, you know with enough experience that you don't. It's not comfortable, but it is comforting to know that you'll still be alive after the anxiety passes.

Anxiety may have played a major role in your life, or perhaps it only bothers you from time to time, or somewhere in between. Either way, it's something to work on because feelings of anxiety only hinder your ability to move forward and enjoy life more. We laugh, and cry; we also live and die. There's a Mexican folk song which says "ay yay ya yaay, canta y no llores," which means sing and don't cry. While you don't have to sing, the singing part could be laughing or enjoying living. If you don't do these things, there's that possibility that you'll cry. Crying doesn't have to actually mean crying; it can be feeling sad or depressed as life is full of ups and downs. There are many surprises along the way. Everything may be perfect today, but tomorrow may bring a challenge that throws you for a loop, something you didn't expect or want. These are the times that could make us sad or cry. If you are not feeling that emotion at this moment, then enjoy what you have, appreciate the peace, love, prosperity, and special moments in your life so that even when things feel glum, you can find something good in it. Anxiety can always knock on your door and say "Hi, want to play?" You have to choose whether to open the door or say "no, thank you, I'll handle my emotions in a different way with grace and peace." Anxiety isn't bad; it's just not productive. It serves a purpose when it activates fight or flight (chicken or egg). When you have to fight or run, use it until the threat is over; if it's trying to be your friend, let it go; anxiety is not your friend, it's a tool.

We've learned many ways to deal with anxiety, and what is effective for one may not be effective for another. Keep in mind we are all unique individuals. Try each one until you feel the metaphorical "click." Self-hypnosis, meditation, releasing, and being more present are just a few. When you say "this is the one," that's what you stick with. If you're using a technique and it loses its effectiveness, or you feel you're not getting the same result as you used to, move on to another one. Each technique can push you forward, but one may thrust you to the finish line. On the other hand, you may find that each technique you learn can do wonders. It all depends on how you react to them. If you do hypnotherapy, it can make an incredible impact, but if it doesn't, move on to the next method and keep using each one you can get your hands on until you get the "click." Something has to work, and if you started with or are on medication, it's okay. Use what you've learned so that you can take control working deeper than just manipulating brain or body chemistry. Your goal is not to be on meds for the rest of your life; your goal is to be free, free from anxiety and medication. I'm sure no doctor would disagree with me. No doctor wants you to be on medication for the rest of your life. They want you to use it in order to help, and if you don't need them anymore, no problem, even better.

Remember to create good problems in your life. You'll need them now that you understand that the role of our ego is to exist and keep its existence going by solving some difficulty in life. It makes us feel wanted, needed, and useful, but don't create bad problems; create good ones. Be deliberate in your problem creation so that you can solve them, and even if it tires you out, you'll feel a sense of satisfaction from it. If your mind has created a good problem, then you'll keep it busy preventing it from creating a bad one.

Live. If you haven't already, come to the realization that you are going to either live your life or you are going to die it. The Bible says "Choose Life!" Those are wise words because we often times believe that we don't have a choice. Sometimes we don't, but often times we do. Here we are being told to actually make the choice, how powerful! When you think you don't have a choice, ask yourself "Do I have a choice in this?" "What can I do to feel better?" "What path should I take to make my life improve?" Sometimes people say "but I have no choice!" Many times they do, so be truthful to yourself. We may not always be truthful to others, but we can't lie to ourselves.

Finally, keep in mind that living this life is your experience. You get one shot at it and no other. Until now, if it's been filled with fear, worry, nervousness, or anxiety come to the realization that these moments of worry have only robbed you of the precious time you've been given to enjoy life and be productive. You can never recuperate those moments but you can use the ones you have left to live free from these emotions, and become a better version of you. You deserve it! You're not living a better life for your family, friends, co-workers, or loved ones. They will no doubt benefit, but you ultimately benefit the most. You are living a better life for you.

I sincerely hope that this work has helped you improve your life and rid yourself of anxiety, or at the very least got you started on the path. Thank you for your interest and taking the time to read it; I am truly honored that you chose to spend time with me. In this work I shared my past journey with you because the experiences I had were a great teacher on what worked for me, and many others who came seeking my advice or help. I was excited writing this book and continue being excited as I wait to hear the stories that have to share about your freedom from anxiety. I can't wait.

Coming Soon

When Anxiety Wants to Play Workbook. Using the techniques learned in this book, learn how to apply your techniques on a daily basis to turn up the volume on obliterating anxiety from your life.

Please leave a positive review and your thoughts on this book as it helps me and others to rid themselves of anxiety. Thank you. Thank you. Thank you.